THE
GENTLE
ART OF
BLESSING

9/21 Introduction – p. 34

9/2 Chapters 4, 5, 6

10/5 Chapters 7, 8, 9, 10

11/16 Chapters 11, 12, 13

Holy Energy

THE GENTLE ART OF BLESSING

A Simple Practice That
Will Transform You and Your World

PIERRE PRADERVAND

ATRIA PAPERBACK
New York London Toronto Sydney

BEYOND WORDS
Hillsboro, Oregon

ATRIA PAPERBACK
A Division of Simon & Schuster, Inc.
1230 Avenue of the Americas
New York, NY 10020

BEYOND WORDS
20827 N.W. Cornell Road, Suite 500
Hillsboro, Oregon 97124-9808
503-531-8700 / 503-531-8773 fax
www.beyondword.com

Managing editor: Lindsay S. Brown
Editor: Julie Steigerwaldt
Copyeditor: Ali McCart
Proofreader: Marvin Moore
Design: Devon Smith
Composition: William H. Brunson Typography Services

First Atria Paperback/Beyond Words trade paperback edition November 2009

For more information about special discounts for bulk purchases,
please contact Simon & Schuster Special Sales at 1-866-506-1949 or
business@simonandschuster.com.

The Simon & Schuster Speakers Bureau can bring authors to your live event.
For more information or to book an event, contact the Simon & Schuster Speakers
Bureau at 1-866-248-3049 or visit our website at www.simonspeakers.com.

Manufactured in the United States of America

10 9 8 7

Library of Congress Cataloging-in-Publication Data:

Pradervand, Pierre.
[Vivre sa spiritualité au quotidien. English]
The gentle art of blessing : a simple practice that will transform you and your world /
Pierre Pradervand. — 1st Atria Paperback/Beyond Words trade pbk. ed.
p. cm.
Includes bibliographical references.
1. Blessing and cursing. 2. Benediction. 3. Love. 4. Forgiveness. I. Title.
BL560.P7313 2009
203'.8—dc22

2009020532

ISBN: 978-1-58270-242-1
ISBN: 978-1-43915-363-5 (ebook)

The corporate mission of Beyond Words Publishing, Inc.: *Inspire to Integrity*

To **Elly**, my companion, friend, wife, and morning.

> **Morning:** *freshness, openness, gratitude, inspiration, newness, alertness, expectation of good, wakefulness, fresh beginning, purity, threshold, (re)birth, joy, innocence, wonder.*

Thank you for the daily wonder and endless morning you are in my life. Thank you for being my teacher.

I also dedicate this book to my friend **Roger W. McGowen**, who for over twenty-two years has been on death row for a crime many believe he did not commit. He was transferred in March 2000 to a high security unit in Livingston, Texas.

Thank you, Roger, for our deep sharing. Thank you for being a shining example of extraordinary courage, goodness, and resilience in a totally inhumane surrounding. May God bless you.

Thy days shall be clearer than the noonday,
thou shalt shine forth,
thou shalt be as the morning.

JOB 11:17

CONTENTS

A Note from the Publisher   ix

Acknowledgments   xi

Introduction   xiii

1   How It All Started   1

2   A History of Blessing   17

3   A Universe of Spiritual Laws   25

4   The Law of Positive Expectations   35

5   The Law of Right Returns   41

6   The Golden Rule   61

7   The Law of Unconditional Love   77

8   The Law of Universal Harmony   89

9   The Deeper Meaning of the Art of Blessing   103

10   A New Way of Seeing and Believing   109

11   Seeing the Hidden Good   123

12   Don't Forget to Bless Yourself   129

13   Blessing as a Spiritual Path   147

Blessings for Everyday Life   163

Epilogue: Blessing—A Practice That Heals   179

Letters and Emails   187

Suggested Reading   199

A Note from the Publisher

About a year ago I received a call from an overseas book distributor. He wanted to bring my attention to a book about blessing, which had sold more copies than a typical *New York Times* bestseller. He felt it was very special and thought we could do a good job bringing it to a wide readership. When I read *The Gentle Art of Blessing*, I couldn't have agreed more.

The book you hold in your hands first appeared as a collection of wonderful words on blessing that the author passed around to his friends, family, and acquaintances. The response was overwhelming, and soon that circle grew to include strangers from around the globe. The first version was published in French in 1998 and later in English in 2003. When we expressed our interest in the book to its first English language publisher, they saw the importance of bringing this message to a broader audience.

With this edition, we hope to touch as many lives as possible with Pierre's profound teachings on the power of blessing. After publishing *The Secret*, whose message of gratitude struck a chord with millions of people, I see in this book the concept of gratitude taken to the next level. This active spiritual practice is a silent revolution, even more important in these challenging times. It truly has the power to connect hearts around the world.

Through this book you will also have the privilege of knowing Pierre, a gentle soul with a vital message for humanity. Please listen carefully.

Cynthia Black

Cynthia Black
Editor in Chief
Beyond Words Publishing

ACKNOWLEDGMENTS

My thanks go Candace Jagel, Bunny McBride, and Susan Remkus, for their most able editing and especially for weeding out my Gallicisms.

I especially wish to thank Cynthia Black and Richard Cohn of Beyond Words Publishing for having believed in the book, and also Lindsday S. Brown, the managing editor, for having steered the book so capably and thoughtfully through all the steps till publication, and Julie Steigerwaldt and Ali McCart for their very able, careful, and sensitive editing, which substantially enhanced the flow and readability.

INTRODUCTION

Blessing has been a spiritual practice of humankind since time immemorial. The ritualized form of blessing that usually concludes many Christian religious ceremonies is only one of the many forms of blessing found across almost all cultures. But far from being simply a ritual that punctuates religious ceremonies, the practice of blessing has the power to enrich your life in ways you never dreamed possible, ways that I have experienced personally.

This book is born of a spiritual experience that profoundly marked my life and enabled me to discover the deep meaning of the act of blessing. Blessing rests on spiritual laws that each of us can discover so that we may live better and more fully. My own experience reinforced my intuitive sense that these spiritual laws, described in the great spiritual teachings of humanity a long time ago, constitute the very basis of our living in the universe—often without our knowledge. They are as precise and efficient as the laws of the physical world, and the discovery of these laws could be one of the greatest breakthroughs of the new millennium. It would give an extraordinary impetus to the evolution of human consciousness, of individuals and nations. You will see that by blessing, you begin living your life in alignment with these spiritual laws. From there, untold rewards await, including lasting joy, a sense of renewal, and peace within.

I have not written these pages as a professional or a master in the field of spirituality or religion. During my whole career, I have been committed to the creation of a world with a little more justice and compassion, a world that works for all (nature included). For many years, this commitment was lived out in the field of sociological research and international development, then through the trainings I gave for the elderly unemployed and those living on a minimal income. More recently, I live this commitment through workshops I give to people from all walks of life about achieving more value-centered, holistic lives.

Very early in my career, an incident alerted me to the fact that it is useless to attempt to transform social, political, and economic structures if we do not also transform people's hearts. In the mid-sixties, I was working as a sociologist in Algeria, one of the rare developing countries to have won its independence after a long, hard, and often ferocious war of liberation. The head of state of the country was a general who had imprisoned the president appointed at independence. All legal opposition was forbidden, but clandestine opposition groups still existed.

I was responsible for a team of interviewers undertaking a nationwide attitude survey. One of the interviewers had contacts with the opposition. He shared with me that a friend of his had been tortured in a police station exactly where his torturer had himself been tortured by the former colonial army.

I was deeply disturbed that someone who had been tortured could turn around and inflict that kind of pain on another person. I had come to this country out of political idealism, because it had undergone a "real" revolution. Yes, the material structures of the administration, economy, and legal system had been overturned, but the torturer's behavior showed me that the hearts of those who ran the country had apparently not changed in the same measure. To effect true change, I realized, there must be a transformation within.

This was the point of departure of a lifelong reflection that culminates, many years later, with this book. It never would have been written without a short sentence pronounced by Dr. Gerald G. Jampolsky, founder of the internationally known Center for Attitudinal Healing in Tiburon, California, and author of *Forgiveness* and *Love Is Letting Go of Fear*. He uttered the first sentence in a lecture given with his wife, Diane Cirincione, PhD, at the University of Geneva, Switzerland, in the early nineties: "Each time I go to my center, it is to heal myself." This made me understand that we do not need to be a master to help others and that we always have something to give and share, however modest our achievements.

Another idea that gave me the courage to embark on this venture was the well-known saying that we teach what we most need to learn. I write this book as an apprentice on the path of blessing, and I continue learning lessons in this field every day.

My work has taught me that unemployed people begin to really listen when they discover that the person talking to them has also experienced unemployment. We identify more easily with someone who is struggling like us, and this realization was the final impetus to write this book. Having been unemployed myself for a long period, and with no unemployment compensation, I had much greater credibility in their eyes than someone who would have spoken from pure theory. So I hope, dear reader, that you will accept this book as the work of an apprentice who shares it with other apprentices, in the spirit of the great Persian Sufi writer

Farid ud-Din Attar's poem "Mantic Uttair." Attar describes a group
of birds that decides to look for their king, the Simorg. After many
adventures they meet again, facing each other in a circle. They
look at each other and lo, they discover that *they* are the Simorg.
The king is in each of them. The kingdom is in each of us.

How redundant to speak of living our spirituality in everyday
life! For either spirituality is lived in everyday life, in the most mundane circumstances—at the office, at the factory, while gardening
or washing the car, in business or married life, while washing dishes,
in suffering and joy—or it has no reason to exist. If the spiritual
path is not lived in the everyday, where will it be lived? Ashrams in
the Himalayas and monasteries in Tuscany may be conducive to
spiritual seeking, but that's not where the majority of us spend most
of our time. Rabbi Hillel is reputed to have said, "If not you, who? If
not now, when?"

What is appealing about the spiritual path, as the American
spiritual teacher Ram Dass has stressed, is that everything is "grist
for the mill." *Absolutely everything*—a traffic jam, an illness, a
theft, a noisy neighbor, a flat tire—becomes an opportunity to
learn, discover, progress, repent, rejoice, unveil, awaken, love
more, and wonder. The smallest detail of life, every single
encounter—be it with a saint or a snail—can sparkle with tender
interest and become aglow with enchantment. That is the real
excitement of the spiritual path, its beauty, depth, joy, and yes, its
fun. Every single event in life can become an opportunity for a
silent "Yes, thank you."

If you cannot live your spiritual path in the subway, in
the middle of a street fight, when facing a major challenge, or
when playing tennis or baseball, you might question its very
use. This book will also demonstrate for you that spirituality is

not a concept to be debated abstractly but a transforming power that has meaning only if it is lived daily.

A Comment on Words

The French writer Georges Bernanos stated that "one of mankind's greatest disgraces was to have to entrust something as precious and subtle as our thoughts to something as unstable and pliable as words." A book that speaks of spirituality and transcendence necessarily mentions words such as *Providence, God, Creator,* and so on. The term *God,* for instance, is only a word that probably corresponds to as many different conceptions as there are human beings. For me, there are immutable spiritual laws that govern the universe. These laws emanate from an unconditionally loving principle of harmony. Some will find it easier to call this principle *God,* while for others the very term could be offensive. Let us not get hung up on words but rather use them as springboards to launch us toward that which is inexpressible. When I use a term such as *Love* with a capital in this book, it will refer to the governing divine Principle or God.

This book suggests a pragmatic, nondenominational, and universal practice of the gentle art of blessing. If certain words bother you, create your own expression, such as *universal life force, infinite law of harmony,* or any other expression that suits you. The wonderful thing about blessing is that even atheists can practice it! A very dear friend of over forty years standing, who at the beginning of one of my workshops on spirituality described herself as a communist-atheist, told me: "Every time you used the word *God,* I replaced it with *life* and all was fine." She has shared this book on blessing freely.

INTRODUCTION

Gandhi once compared God to the summit of a mountain. Each of us reaches that place by a different path. Some trails are straighter than others. But sooner or later, we'll all get there. (And for some, the only *there* is here and now.) As Rabbi François Garai of the Liberal Jewish Community of Geneva, Switzerland, once wrote with delightful humor, "Everyone has his own path to knowing the existence of God. Let us not standardize the way, and may God protect us from all spiritual cloning."

In Patton Boyle's book *Screaming Hawk*, his fictional American Indian teacher, Flying Eagle, tells him: "The truth comes in the silence between the words. It is grasped and experienced with the heart." I hope that you, as a reader of this book, will attempt just that—to listen with your heart to the silence between the words. Listen to the echoes the words evoke in you. Please do not trip on these unstable, plastic symbols. Once more, no truth can be adequately contained in words. Even the most profound spiritual writings of humanity or the clearest explanations of scientists cannot constitute the truth. They are, at best, indicators. Gandhi exclaimed, "My life is my message." Jesus said, "He that *doeth* the truth cometh to the light"—not he or she who preaches or *writes* about it!

Another vitally important distinction is between spirituality and religion. *Spirituality*, which derives from the Latin *spiritus*, meaning "breath," refers to an individual's personal experience of the divine, to her or his spiritual path. Religion usually refers to a collective or group experience, to an organized system of beliefs and creeds, experienced through the medium of a certain institution or structure. A person can be a fervent adherent of a given religion and be totally devoid of any true spirituality as expressed through qualities such as compassion and joy, forgiveness and inspiration. Another person can be a lifelong free thinker, agnostic, or even atheist, and yet constantly live the values and qualities of the spirit.

One might say that religions are human attempts to define the indefinable. Individuals and groups often come to believe their definitions, which are only signposts, and forget the reality toward which these are pointing. Worse, they come to fight over the words on the signposts and forget where they are going!

Organized religion furnishes only *one* context through which eternal truths can be expressed. It resembles crutches: often necessary, but temporary at best. At the present stage of human history and collective level of consciousness, certain forms of organized religion are certainly useful and necessary. The great religions of the world have furnished societies with an ethical dimension indispensable to human progress. But who, if they have the choice, would not prefer to walk without crutches, or to spring from the diving board and swim? This is the reason that for many great spiritual teachings of humanity, truth resides first and foremost in demonstration, in the truth lived, in a state of consciousness, and not in dogmas, rituals, or sacred books. In recent years, I have even started speaking of the practice of blessing as a form of lay spirituality, a practice that can be adopted by almost anyone, of any faith, even agnostics.

It is my hope that reading this book will inspire you to practice the gentle art of blessing in your own unique way. Throughout this book, we will explore the spiritual laws that form the basis of the art of blessing. With new understanding, you will see that blessing helps you live your life in accordance with these universal laws, allowing all their wonderful consequences to flow to you. As it has for me and for hundreds of others who have written to me over the past twenty years, blessing will bring you a deep joy and lasting calm, leading you to a richer, fuller, and happier life. Of one thing I am certain—it will unseal inner fountains of healing and bliss. Once they start to flow, they will grow with every sincere blessing.

1

HOW IT ALL STARTED

Bless them that curse you.

MATTHEW 5:44

A t one point in my career, I was employed in the field of inter-national development, working in the Swiss school system with both students and teachers. During this time I had to make one of the most difficult decisions in my career: keep my job but accept a situation that violated the most elementary professional ethics, or quit. (I learned later that the people who put me in this situation were actively banking on my leaving!)

So, rather than commit moral hara-kiri, I quit.

In the following weeks, I developed a deep-seated and all-consuming resentment such as I had never experienced before against the people who had put me in this impossible situation. When I awoke in the morning, my first thought was of them. As I showered, as I walked along the streets, as I went shopping or jogging, this resentment obsessed me, eating me up, draining my energy and robbing me of all peace. I was literally being poisoned. I knew I was harming myself, but despite hours of meditation, prayer, and spiritual study, this obsession clung to me. I felt and behaved like a total victim!

Then one day, a statement in Jesus's Sermon on the Mount struck me as never before: "Bless them that curse you" (Matthew 5:44). Suddenly, everything became clear. This is what I had to do. Bless my former "persecutors." Right then and there, I started to bless them in every way imaginable: in their health and their joy, their finances and their work, their family relations and their peace, their abundance and their goodness. The ways to bless them were endless. By *blessing*, I mean wishing from the bottom of the heart, in total sincerity, the very best for those people—their complete fulfillment and deepest happiness. For instance, if a friend is in a state of deep depression, I will bless them in their peace, joy, and wholeness, which is hidden to the material eyes but very present at another level of their being.

This is the most important dimension of blessing: sincerity that comes from the heart. This is the power that transforms and heals, elevates and restores. It is the very antipode of a stereotyped ritual. Spontaneous blessing is a flowing fountain that, like a mountain stream, cascades and sings. It expresses perpetual *morning*—defined as freshness, openness, gratitude, inspiration, newness, alertness, expectation of good, wakefulness, fresh beginning, purity, threshold, (re)birth, joy, innocence, wonder.

At first, these blessings were a conscious decision activated by my will but born of a sincere spiritual intention to heal my thinking. The key factor was the intention. Slowly, the blessings moved from being an act of the will to a yearning of the heart—because the act of blessing comes essentially from the heart.

I blessed those people all day long—when I was brushing my teeth, jogging, on my way to the post office or supermarket, washing dishes, and before falling asleep—individually and silently. This process of blessing continued for quite a few years.

After a few months of this practice of blessing, one day, quite spontaneously, I started blessing people in the street, on the bus, at the post office, or when I stood in lines. At the beginning of this wonderful discovery, I would sometimes walk the whole length of a plane or train just for the joy of silently blessing the travelers—unreservedly and unconditionally. This gentle art of blessing became a silent song, the driving power of my spiritual life, a bit like the *cantus firmus* of a Bach cantata. Little by little, blessing people became one of the greatest joys of my life—and it still is now, after many years of practice. I have found it to be one of the most efficient ways of staying spiritually centered and of freeing my thoughts from negativity, criticism, and judgment. Learning more about the spiritual laws that govern the universe, which we'll discuss in the chapters ahead, revealed to me why blessing had this effect.

I never received any roses from my former employer, nor even the slightest expression of regret. Rather, I have received roses from life. By the armful.

BLESSINGS RETURNED

Thanks to this gentle art, I started having rather amazing experiences. One such incident occurred when in my position as a volunteer in a world campaign against hunger, I organized a benefit concert on World Food Day (October 16), the proceeds of which were to be sent to several peasant-farmer groups in southern

Senegal. An Afro-Caribbean orchestra managed by a friend of mine was offering its services free of charge for the concert, which had been advertised both on the radio and in local newspapers. The technician of the large college hall where the concert was to be held showed, for no apparent reason, immense hostility toward the project from the start. He wanted nothing to do with it. We even had to bring in a second technician to handle the sound system and lighting.

Two hours before the concert, the first technician took nearly all the microphones off the stage. My friend was categorical: impossible to have only two mikes for a ten-person orchestra with vocalists! So we went to see the technician. Right from the beginning of our discussion, he maintained his hostility. My initial reaction was anger, but just as quickly I knew anger would not heal the situation. And the public was to arrive in less than two hours! So as the technician argued with my friend, I silently started blessing him: in his goodness, his abundance, his integrity, his health, and his relationships—in every way I could imagine. Suddenly, between two sentences, his attitude changed completely. Where a few seconds earlier we had seen a hate-filled expression, suddenly a beautiful smile appeared. He went to his lab, came back with a pile of mikes, recommended the best ones to my friend, and wished us a wonderful evening.

On another occasion, I was finishing a book chronicling my research on grassroots development in Africa, which had involved visiting over one hundred villages all over the continent. I had undertaken this research as an act of faith, with the desire to correct the erroneous, negative picture of Africa most people have. I trusted that if I wrote a good book, I would find a publisher.

4

As I was concluding the writing, I met a person who had experience in publishing in France. We became instant friends, and he suggested I send him the finished manuscript, offering to forward it to a friend in a good publishing house. Once finished, I phoned to say I was about to send him the manuscript. I also mentioned that I had a literary agent, as I hoped to publish the book in other languages too. The minute I mentioned the term *literary agent*, he exploded with the most vulgar expletives. "As long as you have an agent, don't count on me," he said, slamming down the phone. Taken aback, I thought he must have had a painful experience with a literary agent.

Because I didn't want to keep in mind a negative picture of my new friend, every time he crossed my mind in the following days, I blessed him. About ten days later, he called, as if nothing had happened, to suggest that I tell my agent to send the manuscript to his friend who worked as director of a publishing house. He would write to this person and recommend my book.

The result was that the book was accepted immediately for publication by an excellent publisher. My agent told me that in twenty years in this field, she had never seen a book published so quickly. At the last minute, the publishing house even advanced the date of publication so that the book could appear in time for an international book fair. My friend was able to obtain a preface for the book by a leading European politician, who was highly respected for his knowledge of Africa. I could not have dreamed for more!

THE GENTLE ART OF BLESSING

One day, about seven months after starting the practice of blessing, I was preparing a talk, "Healing the World," for an international youth meeting in Zürich, Switzerland, when suddenly I was overwhelmed by an inspiration to record the practice of blessing that I had been living. I felt literally like a scribe under dictation, so much so that my hand had difficulty keeping up with the ideas that flowed into my mind. What follows is the result of that inspiration, which describes blessing as a spiritual practice and offers guidelines for incorporating the art into your everyday life.

❧ On awakening, bless this day, for it is already full of unseen good which your blessings will call forth, for to bless is to acknowledge the unlimited good that is embedded in the texture of the universe and awaiting each and all.

❧ On passing people in the street, on the bus, in places of work and play, bless them. The peace of your blessing will accompany them on their way, and its aura will be a light on their path.

❧ On meeting people and talking to them, bless them in their health, their work, their joy, their relationship to the universe, themselves, and others. Bless them in their abundance and their finances, bless them in every conceivable way, for such blessings not only sow seeds of healing but one day will spring forth as flowers in the waste places of your own life.

❧ As you walk, bless the city in which you live, its government and teachers, its nurses and street sweepers, its children and bankers, its priests and prostitutes. The minute anyone expresses the least aggression or unkindness to you, respond with a blessing. Bless them totally, sincerely, joyfully—for such blessings are a shield that protects them from the ignorance of their misdeed and deflects the arrow that was aimed at you.

🍂 To bless means to wish, unconditionally and from the deepest chamber of your heart, unrestricted good for others and events; it means to hallow, to hold in reverence, to behold with awe that which is always a gift from the Creator. He who is hallowed by your blessing is set aside, consecrated, holy, whole. To bless is to invoke divine care upon, to speak or think gratefully for, to confer happiness upon, although we ourselves are never the bestower but simply the joyful witnesses of life's abundance.

🍂 To bless all without distinction is the ultimate form of giving, because those you bless will never know from whence came the sudden ray that burst through the clouds of their skies, and you will rarely be a witness to the sunlight in their lives.

🍂 When something goes completely askew in your day, when some unexpected event upsets your plans—and upsets you—burst into blessing. For life is teaching you a lesson, and the very event you believe to be unwanted, you yourself called forth, so as to learn the lesson you might balk against were you not to bless it. Trials are blessings in disguise, and hosts of angels follow in their path.

🍂 To bless is to acknowledge the omnipresent, universal beauty hidden from material eyes; it is to activate that law of attraction which, from the furthest reaches of the universe, will bring into your life exactly what you need to experience and enjoy.

❧ When you pass a prison, mentally bless its inmates in their innocence and freedom, their gentleness, pure essence, and unconditional forgiveness; for one can only be a prisoner of one's self-image, and a free man can walk unshackled in jail, just as citizens of a free country may be prisoners of the fear lurking within their thoughts.

❧ When you pass a hospital, bless its patients in their present wholeness, for even in their suffering, their wholeness awaits discovery within them. When your eyes behold a man in tears or seemingly broken by life, bless him in his vitality and joy, for the material senses present but the inverted image of the ultimate splendor and perfection that only the inner eye beholds.

❧ It is impossible to bless and judge at the same time. So hold constantly as a deep, hallowed, intoned thought the desire to bless, for truly then shall you become a peacemaker, and one day you shall behold, everywhere, the very face of God.

❧ P.S. And of course, above all, do not forget to bless the utterly beautiful person *you* are.

In the following months, I shared this short text with friends in different countries. As months turned into years, I started receiving letters and phone calls from all around the world, mostly from people I had never met.

A mother in a small town in Burkina Faso, West Africa, wrote, "As a result of studying your text, we bless those who harm us and pray for them." Mahmoudou, a man who works at the grassroots with farmers in the Mopti region of Mali, a western neighbor of Burkina Faso, shared his experience of blessing in a moving letter:

I have started to turn blessing into an everyday experience, in all situations. It has become part of my very marrow. And each day, it fills me more and more. It has started to sharpen my sense of sharing, of justice, of equity and solidarity. I am becoming more patient, tolerant, forbearing, understanding— and sensitive to everything that affects my neighbor. To begin with, I did not understand, because it was at the same time very difficult and very easy to forgive someone who had deliberately harmed me. Then I understood that I only needed to master my heart. This means that all depends on the state of mind we have toward things. May Allah, who is Supreme Wisdom, grant us a loving state of mind. I thank you sincerely. May Allah reward you. When I bless someone who is suffering physically, morally, or materially, I am filled with a comforting breath which does me good and makes me strong and serene. I have distributed your text all around me and even far off.

What a rich harvest Mahmoudou received because he gave his heart and soul to the practice of blessing! Later, he wrote me, "I discussed your text with the elders of the village, and these wise men all approved it, saying that he who wants to protect himself from his enemy's arrow must have the courage to face him and do him good, with a smile on his face and in the heart. In this way, the arrow will be deflected and will fall on the arid soil."

A couple in California who run self-development workshops wrote to say they were using the text with hundreds of people. A spiritual healer on the Isle of Wight, Great Britain, wrote, "*The Gentle Art of Blessing* is snowballing and can only unite people of all walks of life in a link of peace. It touches receptive hearts, bringing forth the goodness that is inherent in each one." She mentioned that she had given it to shopkeepers and hairdressers and "the Mother Superior of a Catholic convent who was so inspired by it she made copies for all the nuns in her convent."

A friend sent the text to an acquaintance of his in Poland. She replied,

> The Gentle Art of Blessing *arrived just at the right moment, and I have had the opportunity to apply it. Yes, truly "Life is teaching you a lesson" (as the text says). I had some "visitors" at my summer house. They looted all the rooms, leaving an incredible mess. I blessed them. They helped themselves to my food. I blessed them. They also stole my camera, my Swiss axe, my alarm clock. I blessed them. They broke a window and two doors. I blessed them. They do not have a home. I do. So I blessed them. They are now in prison, having raided in like manner fifteen houses. "When you pass a prison, mentally bless its inmates." I blessed them again. This weekend, I will be very busy—blessing.*

A woman in Lewiston, Maine, wrote, "This is an essay that, when deeply contemplated, can turn us completely away from selfish cares and interests. You will not be surprised, therefore, when I say it made me say to myself, I cannot hope to enter into the kingdom of heaven until I am ready to take everyone else in with me."

A participant in the "Recreating Your Life" workshops I give each summer, high up in the Swiss Alps, wrote, "I use blessings with interest, surprise, and pleasure. I realized that I often had a rather mocking way of considering people and that I could transform that attitude into blessings. I like that!"

Roger, to whom this book is co-dedicated and who has been twenty-two years on death row in Texas for a crime he never committed, described the terrible prison conditions, the harassment by the wardens, the freezing cold cells. He then wrote,

> I was ready to explode. I prayed, but for some reason, I could not find comfort in my prayers. Finally, at night, before I went to bed, I read the beginning parts of your book and I can tell you now that it changed my thought process. After reading, I just started asking God to bless all of these people, to bless them and their families, to bless them in their financial life, their spiritual life, every aspect of their lives. And . . . very gently, very slowly, the weight began to lift from my shoulders, not all at once, but gradually. And now, every morning, when I wake up, the first thing I do is bless them, and again in the middle of the day, and before I go to sleep at night.

Jean-Hilaire, an inmate from Cameroon whom I visited weekly as a volunteer at the Geneva penitentiary, wrote, "Since reading *The Gentle Art of Blessing*, I feel deep inside me a power and an extraordinary ability to say: We can change men, we can repaint the world with enthusiasm and hope."

This overwhelming response told me that there was something to this practice. It had been missing from people's lives. Perhaps people had gotten away from the practice, or never learned it to begin with. Many of us have been told of the benefits of gratitude, but the art of blessing is something more: extending sincere, benevolent wishes from the bottom of our heart to another person. For whatever reason, one thing was certain: bringing it into people's lives was having a definite impact.

EVERYDAY BLESSING

Many spiritual teachings and numerous mystics stress the importance for the spiritual disciple to develop a constant awareness of the divine. The Vietnamese Buddhist teacher Thich Nhat Hanh suggests this be done by striving to live in the present. One of the great classics of Christian mysticism, *The Practice of the Presence of God* by Brother Lawrence, a seventeenth-century Cistercian French monk who worked in the monastery kitchen, stresses this practice as a privileged way of developing such awareness. Such practices may not be excessively difficult in an ashram in the Himalayas, a monastery in Montana, or with fellow pilgrims during the Muslim hajj to Mecca—or even during your morning meditation at home in Toronto, London, or Manhattan. But how do you keep such a spiritual awareness when you are alone in an elevator with someone having an epileptic seizure? How do you keep your spiritual poise during a transatlantic flight with the baby in the seat behind you crying its heart out? How do you keep your calm when someone insults you without reason? How do you feel love rather than pity in a refugee camp with hundreds of starving children pulling at your clothes?

The practice of blessing is a simple way to develop a constantly centered awareness. It is also a tool for growing in universal love and avoiding judgment. When you bless all those you meet in their total happiness and true integrity, without the slightest concern for their appearance, expression, race, class, sex, or any other label, when you wish them the very best from your innermost being, it is impossible for your heart not to expand. From a narrow cubicle, it will become a temple without walls.

A constant reminder of spiritual masters is that you cannot grow spiritually if you are burdened mentally by the habit of judging others. But do not take my word for it, try it for yourself. Try to systematically replace every single thought of judgment with blessing—especially for that fellow at the office who drives you out of your wits!

I love what spiritual philosopher David Spangler writes in his beautiful book *Blessing: The Art and the Practice*:

> *Blessing is not a technique we perform but a presence we embody. It is not an act we do to someone or something, but a relationship we form with them that enables us all to be embraced in the presence of an unobstructed world.*

He adds that a blessing can take many shapes—a hug, a tone of voice, a word or glance. What makes it a blessing is the spirit we bring to it.

Create your own ways of blessing. There are no set formulas. My way of blessing has changed over the years. At the present, when I bless people in the street, on the bus, or anywhere, I say in my heart: "Namaste! I love you. I bless you in your divine perfection and total happiness." (*Namaste* is a Sanskrit expression meaning "I acknowledge the divine in you.") I try to really feel the love, and this forces me to look beyond the physical appearance, which is not always very inviting, to the hidden, harmonious, perfect spiritual reality behind.

Try blessing. You will be the first to benefit!

I'd like to share with you the outcome of the story that began this chapter. A few years ago, by one of the "chance" encounters Providence sets up for us with perfect synchronicity, at a meeting of an organization we both belonged to, I happened to encounter the person who had masterminded the ugly situation that caused me to quit my job and ultimately led me to discover the art of blessing. I cannot find words to express the incredible wave of joy that flooded me, or the deep love—and especially, gratitude—I felt for this man. It was one of the most powerful moments of deep joy I have ever known. For days, this joy was to stay with me. Even as I write about it now, the feeling of joy comes back to me.

Here was the man who apparently had caused me to lose a job I thoroughly enjoyed, where I had immense freedom and felt very useful to society—and all I could feel was deep gratitude welling up from my soul.

This experience was a milestone in enabling me to feel (not to know or believe, but really to *feel*) that truly, there was a perfect plan for my life—that whatever happened to me, it would always end up being in my best interest if my life stayed rooted in total sincerity and the integrity of being described in this book.

Somewhere, even our enemies (*especially* our enemies!)— be they circumstances or people—are the best friends of our growth.

What an amazing universe we live in!

On Your Path to Blessing

When is the last time you blessed someone?
Who in your past might it help you to bless?
Who in your present might it help you to bless?
Could blessing help you live more fully in the
* present?*

2
A HISTORY OF BLESSING

Blessed shalt thou be when thou comest in,
and blessed shalt thou be when thou goest out . . .
—DEUTERONOMY 28:6

Blessing is a millennial art. In the religious context, blessings have existed throughout centuries across almost all cultures. Lay forms of blessings also permeate our culture in the form of housewarming parties, the European custom of mounting an evergreen on the gable of a new house once the roof has been erected, the rice thrown on newlyweds, and so on. In some regions of the Swiss Alps, shepherds today sing out a blessing through a very primitive kind of wooden megaphone to the four cardinal directions. North American Indians have tribal blessings for numerous occasions.

Caitlín Matthews, in her book *The Little Book of Celtic Blessings*, shows that blessings have long been used in all circumstances of life. Many blessings rest on the understanding that there exists a universal power, a fundamental principle of harmony governing all things, to which people may appeal. Here, for instance, is "Blessing for a Lover":

> *You are the star of each night,*
> *You are the brightness of every morning,*
> *You are the story of each guest,*
> *You are the report of every land.*
>
> *No evil shall befall you. On hill nor bank,*
> *In field or valley, On mountain or in glen.*
>
> *Neither above nor below, Neither in sea*
> *Nor on shore,*
> *In skies above, Nor in the depths.*
>
> *You are the kernel of my heart,*
> *You are the face of my sun,*
> *You are the harp of my music,*
> *You are the crown of my company.*

In numerous preindustrial cultures, blessings accompanied all the important activities of life: sowing and reaping, hunting and fishing, crafts production and the preparation of meals, for example. The Old Testament brims with acts of blessing (also giving examples of its opposite, cursing). For instance, in the book of Numbers it is reported that when the Israelites were returning to their homeland, King Balak attempted to hire the services of a great seer of the time, Balaam, to curse them. Balaam, it is said, received God's order to do the exact contrary, i.e., bless the Israelites, which deeply frustrated the king. The *very first thing*

God Herself did after creating man and woman was bless them (Genesis 1:28).[1]

In the book of Deuteronomy (30:19), the writer draws a parallel between the act of blessing and life itself, and also between cursing and death. "I have set before you life and death, blessing and cursing: therefore choose life, that both thou and thy seed may live." The limited, personal sense of blessing prevalent during biblical times, however, meant that the blessing which Jacob "stole" from his brother Esau could no longer be bestowed upon the latter, because it had already been "given" away—as if true blessings could possibly be limited!

The following biblical passage from Deuteronomy 28:3–8 stresses beautifully—and poetically—how concretely blessing applies to every situation in life:

> *Blessed shalt thou be in the city, and blessed shalt thou be in the field. Blessed shall be the fruit of thy body, and the fruit of thy ground, and the fruit of thy cattle, the increase of thy kine, and the flocks of thy sheep. Blessed shall be thy basket and thy store.*
>
> *Blessed shalt thou be when thou comest in, and blessed shalt thou be when thou goest out. . . . The Lord shall command the blessing upon thee in thy storehouses, and in all that thou settest thine hand unto; and he shall bless thee in the land which the Lord thy God giveth thee.*

The "Lord thy God" is the principle of unconditional love upholding the universe, and the "land" can also refer to a state of consciousness. It is our state of consciousness that determines whether and how we receive these blessings. They are at all times simply pouring down onto us, so immense is the generosity of life.

As these brief examples show, blessings are as old as humanity itself, stretching across religions and cultures, and through all circumstances of life.

ANCIENT BLESSINGS

The ancient spiritual teachers understood the extraordinary power of thoughts—both good or bad—that we have only started to rediscover. Thoughts can very literally give life or kill. Thus the book of Exodus 21:17 condemns to death he who has cursed his parents. And in the struggle between Jacob and the angel at Peniel in Genesis 32, Jacob refuses to let go of the angel before the angel blesses him. (This story is to be interpreted in its symbolical sense as the new birth of Jacob, who becomes aware of his spiritual identity; hence his change of name, which indicates his awareness of his divine nature.)

That a practice such as blessing could be so universally widespread in almost all cultures, probably since the beginning of time, stresses an important factor: the slow awakening of humanity to a fundamental reality which could be called the *law of the attraction of good,* a concept we will explore in greater detail in the coming pages.

At its deepest level, blessing implies a sense of the sacred, of some hidden abundance available to those who open themselves up to it through this practice, of some unseen power available to protect and make whole. Most often, it refers to good received from a deity through certain practices, and that is probably its most widely accepted sense.

For instance, in the Maha Mangala Sutta, the Buddha lists the thirty-eight highest blessings for a Buddhist, such as associating with the wise, right self-guidance, cherishing one's wife or partner, being generous, expressing contentment and gratitude, having an undefiled mind, and so on. By practicing these blessings, we ourselves are blessed and also those around us.

It is much less known that in Judaism, one of the most widespread spiritual practices in the world, blessing constitutes the roots of its practice, its fundamental grounding. The very first chapter of Genesis states that God blessed the creatures she had just brought to life, man and woman. Thus blessing is renewed to Abraham, and again to Moses. The blessings received from God constitute the very center of Jewish practice, to the extent that a leading Jewish scholar, Rabbi Walter Homolka, has spoken of a culture of blessing which extends far beyond the prayer service to the smallest acts of everyday life. (This practice is not unlike the Buddhist "gathas", which are declarations of mindfulness attached to the most mundane activities). In the Hebrew Bible, it is not only God who blesses her creatures, but human beings as well who bless their Creator.

The Mishna—the codification of Jewish religious law which was written circa 200 CE—begins with a section on blessings (B'rachot, from the word B'racha, the Hebrew term for blessing). Baruch means "[he who is] blessed." Rabbi Meir, in the second century of this era, stated that a Jew should pray one hundred blessings a day. The B'racha is the center of the daily liturgy as well as of individual and family spirituality.

In his radical redefinition of many basic spiritual concepts, Jesus gives fresh meaning to the act of blessing. In the Beatitudes, he shows that blessedness is the result of living in harmony with the fundamental laws of the universe, some of which are presented in this famous text (Matthew 5:1–12). For instance, Jesus indicated that those who had a pure heart would see the divine reflection everywhere. Those who had a clear thought, who refused to split hairs, to intellectualize spiritual truths (the "poor in spirit") would have their hearts filled with and governed by unconditional love, the deeper dimension of the kingdom of God.

Jesus also stressed that numerous blessings, or good, would come the way of those who radiated goodness. "Blessed are the meek: for they shall inherit the earth" (Matthew 5:5). In other words, ultimately, true goodness always triumphs over hate, obscurity, and violence, not because there is any special moral virtue in doing good but because *unconditional love expressed as goodness constitutes the ultimate structure of reality and of the universe.*

However, if there are innumerable references to the blessings received or bestowed by the deity or certain spiritual practices such as the thirty-eight Buddhist blessings mentioned above, or bestowed by priests or holy men or women, there are very few references to what one might call a "lay" practice of blessing such as this book encourages, i.e., the active blessing of others whatever one's religious background or absence of such a background.

The act of blessing triggers some of the fundamental spiritual laws governing the universe. These laws appear to be as rigorous and dependable as the laws of the physical universe, albeit more difficult to verify according to the methodology of modern science. It is therefore important to understand that the art of blessing does not simply mean having a few good words or positive thoughts. When the laws that underpin this practice are understood, blessing can become a powerful tool for good, a means of healing, as my friend Mahmoudou and many others have discovered through its practice.

On Your Path to Blessing

Do you have a favorite blessing from your culture or heritage?

What kinds of daily rituals in your life could benefit from a blessing?

What would you say to bless your home and your family?

NOTE

1. Because I believe that love is the ultimate substance and nature of the infinite Reality humans call God, and because history and culture tend to identify love more as a feminine than a masculine quality—albeit a spiritual quality could not really have gender characteristics—I will use the term *She* rather than *He* to qualify Deity, except when quoting texts where the term appears in the masculine form. It appears ever more clearly that Divinity, whatever its ultimate form, is beyond any gender identification. At the same time, it behooves us to give up thousands of years of theological thinking dominated by male opinion. This will help erode the sexist bias of a great deal of religious literature, and—in Christianity at least, but probably also in Islam and Judaism—the severe image of the Godhead many people still have. Forgiveness will start replacing the fear of punishment, which so often was used to keep believers in their place—totally submissive and unquestioning—as if infinite Love could ever punish.

3

A UNIVERSE OF SPIRITUAL LAWS

*We are at the verge of being forced by physics into accepting the fact
that thought and body cannot be separated.*

Dr. Laurence Doyle

As I stated in the introduction, the act of blessing brings you into alignment with the spiritual laws that govern the universe. Before we take this idea any further, it's necessary to explain just what is meant by spiritual laws and how they differ from other universal laws we may already be familiar with.

By *law* I mean an imperative, universal reality that describes a constant relationship between various phenomena or variables. The universe is governed by laws, which most people call laws of physics, chemistry, physiology, biology, and so on. Human society and technology rest on the assumption of a set of laws governing the universe and reality. Without such laws, the universe would function in a state of anarchy. Modern science would be inconceivable without a framework of such laws. But with a few exceptions, science accepts their existence only on the material—and not the spiritual—level.

Because of this resistance to the idea of spiritual laws, modern science imposes upon itself some very restrictive—and unscientific—blinders. The scientific method represents a certain approach to reality based on experimentation and the capacity to predict certain events on the basis of a given hypothesis. Yet absolutely nothing in the scientific method per se prevents its application to spiritual realities and events. For instance, nothing would prevent a very scientific-minded MD from searching for the causes of an exceptional "spontaneous remission" from late-stage cancer on the spiritual level rather than feeling completely baffled because he sees absolutely no explanation on the physical level. Indeed, a growing body of data in the field of health points to the existence of such spiritual laws.

Among progressive thinkers, for example in the field of medicine, the idea of spiritual laws is gaining in acceptance. As an example of how far we've come, Harvard University organized a series of conferences starting in the mid-nineties, bringing together doctors and healers—including spiritual healers—from around the globe. Here is one of the most prestigious schools of medicine in the world organizing a conference gathering top scientists and religious thinkers to examine, amongst other things, the statistically proven impact of prayer on physical health. This is truly a breakthrough![1]

The scientific approach to reality excludes the idea of a miracle with the connotation of an event that could happen in a gratuitous and unpredictable manner, outside the context or structure of the laws governing the universe. I fully endorse such a stand. However, when in a strictly controlled scientific experiment we can show the statistically significant impact of prayer on a group of cardiac patients, we cannot avoid postulating that a *non-material form of causality is operating*.[2] The idea of a universe where rigorous spiritual laws are operating is beginning to penetrate the scientific community.

OTHER LAWS ARE AT WORK

That spiritual laws have not until now been controlled in a laboratory does not mean that they do not exist. It simply means the proof of their existence must be made in a different manner. An X-ray showing that a fractured bone has healed in a few hours, as the following testimony from Dr. Doyle explains, clearly indicates that laws other than those known by science are at work. It means that our creativity and intelligence must move beyond the self-imposed paradigm or limits of a science based on purely material observation. It implies that we should broaden the scientific method to embrace phenomena and laws which, albeit not measurable in a laboratory, *are no less real* than more visible events and experiments. Because I cannot detect infrared waves or certain sounds with my eyes and ears does not mean they do not exist. It simply means that I need other instruments to track them. Science needs other tools and approaches to explain the growing number of observations that cannot be forced into a material-data straitjacket.

To return to the broken bone story: When I encountered Dr. Laurence Doyle some years ago, he was working for the SETI (Search for Extraterrestrial Intelligence) program of NASA. I was privileged to have long discussions with this brilliant astrophysicist. In a book by John Holmstrom published in the mid-nineties, *When Prayers Are Answered*, Doyle explains the amazing healing he experienced of an open fracture he had sustained as an adolescent.

Doyle was participating in a judo tournament when an opponent seized his finger and bent it back until the bone protruded.

Seeing the bone was broken, Doyle's instructor sent him to the hospital for X-rays. He sat in the emergency room for forty-five minutes, waiting for a doctor. While waiting, he pondered the biblical story of God healing Job when the latter prayed for his friends. He says, "I began talking to and comforting all those people with me in the emergency room until I completely forgot about my hand. When I did look down again, the bone had gone back into place."

Such an adjustment may not be a daily occurrence, but it is something we can accept. What follows is more startling:

> When I got my X-ray the technician said that the bone had been broken, set, and healed already—and that I shouldn't have come to the emergency room at all. The evidence of the broken bone was so obvious that it made the healing extra special: Nobody could argue that it hadn't really been broken. My interpretation of the healing was that your hand exists in your thought. So when your thinking is correct, nothing—including time—can stop the healing process. . . .
>
> We are at the verge of being forced by physics into accepting the fact that thought and body cannot be separated. What are the laws of thought? What are the laws of Mind? That's the renaissance. That's what's coming. And that's why I pray.

We are now in the kind of period described by Thomas Kuhn in *The Structure of Scientific Revolutions*, one of the most important books in the field of the history of science, in which an old paradigm is faced with so many contradictions, it is going to force the formulation of a new one capable of taking the new observations into account in a meaningful way.

SPIRITUALITY WITH A SCIENTIFIC DIMENSION

A spirituality that integrates a scientific dimension does not have to be cold, distant, or impersonal. Mystery, the presence of the sacred, astonished wonder in the face of the infinite and of creation, the fullness of grace, the spontaneity of the childlike soul, the joyous anticipation of the unexpected, a sense of awe—all these can remain intact, vibrant with life. Such a spirituality would simply be enriched with an additional, fundamental dimension. It would in no way be diminished. On the contrary, it would open itself to one more exciting level of consciousness.

And, if the ultimate fabric of the universe, of life itself, is consciousness, who would ever want to be *less* conscious?

LIVE IN TUNE WITH UNIVERSAL LAWS

It is essential to understand that because we humans did not create the laws governing the universe and reality, we cannot play the game of life according to our own rules, any more than a pilot flying an aircraft could suddenly decide to neglect the laws of aerodynamics and fly the plane according to his own rules or fantasy. That would be courting disaster.

Yet it seems that this is just what humanity has been doing for quite some time. We have attempted to invent our own solutions, following our own rules. We have come some way along the path, but at the cost of untold misery for many, for the rules tend to serve the powerful few at the cost of the majority. There has to be a better way.

We don't even have the choice. In fact, it is comforting to realize that, be it individually or collectively, ultimately we will *have* to play the game of life according to the rules of the awesome intelligence that runs this astonishing universe. Is there not a sneaking arrogance in the very idea that we could live life neglecting the laws of creation, which have one aim only: the fulfillment of all creatures living in this universe, including those which in all likelihood live on other planets and in other galaxies?

For instance, if today we have such serious ecological problems, it is clearly because, since the industrial revolution (and even before), we have neglected the laws governing the environment. The only way out for us now is to create a win-win relationship between the environment and the economy, because in the long run, the old win-lose paradigm will cause our demise as a species right along with the demise of the environment. The universal laws exist at all levels, social and individual, as well as environmental and physical.

Before describing these laws, it might be useful to say a few words about how they relate to religion.

A NEW VIEW OF SPIRITUAL LAWS

I was raised in a severe Calvinist church. Its teaching was thoroughly imbued with the idea of human beings' fundamental sinfulness. Every Sunday, I would hear from the pulpit that we were born in evil, inclined toward sin, incapable by ourselves of any good. Life resembled a very steep mountain covered with soap, surrounded by a shark-infested moat (hell). People would climb—or rather slither—on all fours, hanging on to the slightest little protuberance. Progression was painfully slow. And then—whoosh! On Sunday, without pity, we would be pulled back a few lengths. Come Monday, the painstakingly slow ascension would start all over again.

At the top of the mountain sat a very severe personage called God the Father, armed with an unlimited arsenal of lightning rods that He would throw vigorously at poor sinners (and I was always convinced that I was among the worst of the bunch). He held a huge and very impressive black ledger of accounts in which all my sins were carefully recorded, including every single sugar cube I had ever as a child sneaked away from the silver sugar bowl put aside for Sunday coffee. I was persuaded that my debits largely exceeded the rare credits I might have gleaned here and there. This fearsome Divinity had laid down severe laws. Transgressing them entailed certain punishment, the worst of which was to fry forever in a searing place named hell.

Then, years later, having left my family, country, church, I found my own spiritual path, a teaching based on the idea of all-encompassing, completely dependable spiritual laws of harmony that can be applied to the solution of any problem, in any area. It is a true spiritual science. In other words, it upholds that these laws are rigorous and demonstrable (although not necessarily measurable and quantifiable). The menacing and somber Father-accountant slowly yielded to an infinitely good Principle of harmony, endowed with "feminine" as well as "masculine" qualities (I put these two words between quotes because qualities don't have a gender—a man can be as tender as a woman can be strong). The supreme quality of this Principle is unconditional love, which is incapable of punishing, because as the Hebrew prophet Habakuk so clearly describes in the book with his name (1:13), "Thou art of purer eyes than to behold evil." Infinite Love, which is sheer light, is incapable of seeing darkness, because in its presence darkness disappears into its original nothingness. In this newfound understanding, spiritual laws were no longer the plaited whipping ropes designed to deter me from straying, nor were they the guilt-producing punishment and tools they had been in the religion of my youth. Spiritual laws were suddenly seen and experienced as infinitely tender and firm instruments of protection, guidance and, above all, *freedom*.

For many people, the concept of spiritual laws has negative and repressive connotations ("Thou shalt not . . ."). It is always associated with possible punishment. Yet it is my impression that humanity is learning in a gradual and individual process that *the only punishment we can experience is the self-imposed suffering that results from neglecting the spiritual laws that exist solely for our happiness and freedom.* By this perspective, spiritual laws connote guidance and support. They support us in moments of weakness or confusion. They are the most faithful and loving companions of our growth, springboards to a higher vision.

Paradoxically, this concept of spiritual laws represents the highest freedom. It calls upon us to learn how to live life fully, according to the fundamental structure or form governing the universe and reality.

Let us now turn our attention to these spiritual laws and how they guide us in the act of blessing.

On Your Path to Blessing

> *Have you ever had an experience that could*
> *not be described with a concrete, scientific*
> *explanation?*
> *Is a spiritual law any less real than a scientific*
> *law, such as the law of gravity?*
> *Are there any spiritual laws you have seen at*
> *work in your own life?*

NOTES

1. Marquand, Robert, "Healing Role of Spirituality Gains Ground," *Christian Science Monitor*, international edition, Dec. 6, 1995, http://www.csmonitor.com/1995/1206/06013.html. On the Harvard conferences.

2. An abundance of literature on spiritual healing has been published in recent years. For a classic, see Larry Dossey, MD, *Healing Words: The Power of Prayer and the Practice of Medicine* and especially *Reinventing Medicine: Beyond Mind-Body to a New Era of Healing*. Dossey is an international authority in this area. See also Herbert Benson, MD, and Marg Stark, *Timeless Healing: The Power and Biology of Belief*. Probably the first book to attempt a presentation of the rigorous spiritual laws behind spiritual healing is the major study by Mary Baker Eddy, *Science and Health with Key to the Scriptures*. The last hundred pages of this book contain healings of innumerable diseases of all sorts, reached simply by reading the book—a rather remarkable testimony to its contents, to say the least. It is also a confirmation of the existence of *impersonal* spiritual laws which anyone can learn to apply.

4

THE LAW OF POSITIVE
EXPECTATIONS

*On awakening, bless this day, for it is already full of
unseen good which your blessings will call forth,
for to bless is to acknowledge the unlimited good
that is embedded in the texture of the universe
and awaiting each and all.*

"Only that day dawns to which we are awake," wrote Henry David Thoreau. Paraphrasing Thoreau, we could say: By the quality of our expectations and alertness we *choose* the kind of day that dawns in our life. The expectation of good opens us to receive it.

One of the briefest and most powerful expressions of the law of positive expectations is Jesus's statement, "Whatever you pray about and ask for, believe that you *have received* it and it will be yours" (Mark 11:24, J. B. Phillips translation, my emphasis). Prayer is described here not as beseeching some capricious and distant deity whose response is chancy or uncertain but the activation of the universal principle of infinite good which, to manifest itself, depends on the integrity of our motives and an intelligent understanding of the law itself.

That we live in a universe of infinite good—good so abundant that it far exceeds our wildest dreams and most daring leaps of imagination—comes home time and again in the writings of seers and mystics of all times and hues. This abundance is expressed in innumerable ways, from the poetic descriptions of the Sufi mystics to the awed silence of Christian and other seers. Rumi, the great thirteenth-century Sufi poet, wrote,

Behold the garden of the heart, green and fresh
and new, full of rosebuds and cypress and jasmine—
So many leaves that the branches are hidden, so
many roses that the plain and pavilion are concealed!

And the Hebrew prophet Malachi (3:10) echoed, "Prove me now . . . saith the Lord of hosts, if I will not open you the windows of heaven, and pour you out a blessing, that there shall not be room enough to receive it."

One of the most powerful expressions of this abundance in the world's spiritual literature is the reply of the father to his elder son in the well-known parable of the Prodigal Son: "Son, thou art ever with me, and *all that I have* is thine" (Luke 15:31, my emphasis). What a truly extraordinary statement! All the abundance in the universe, everything that constitutes the nature of the ground of being (to use theologian Paul Tillich's powerful metaphor for God), *all* is ours to enjoy.

In other words, and despite all material appearances to the contrary, good is omnipresent. The more we learn to open our mind, our consciousness, to it, the more good manifests itself in our lives. The universe is a place of infinite abundance for all, at all times. This abundance is essentially of a nonmaterial nature but expresses itself in whatever form necessary to meet our true needs, if only we follow the laws that enable us to have access— whether those needs include a job, a companion, finances, a home, rest, food.

All wealth or material invention, every single discovery, whatever it may be, starts with an idea. And by definition, ideas are infinite. How many unemployed—including on occasion the writer of these pages—have found their salvation not in unemployment compensation, which often barely enables survival, but in creativity, which gives birth to projects that generate abundance for them and often for many others? For if we claim good with a pure motive and trust that it will appear, good, indeed, will manifest itself.

If you find the explanation of this law difficult to accept, take it simply as a working hypothesis to test in your life. Have a completely pragmatic attitude toward it. Do not accept anything this book speaks about until you have proved it for yourself. For if every single event and structure in the universe is run by laws— which is the premise of this book—then we can have toward these laws an experimental attitude, almost like that of a scientist in a lab, rather than a mystical attitude or one of blind belief.

AFFIRMING GOOD ALL DAY LONG

One of the most wonderful dimensions of this art of blessing is that you can practice it all day long, whatever activity is part of your day: eating, exercising, mowing the lawn, walking in the street or driving, running an important business meeting or a mothers' club, teaching, the intimacy of married love, taking your morning shower—you name it. As a matter of fact, after twenty-two years of

joyful practice, I can't think of a single normal experience in life—
and I really mean a single one—from which blessing would be
excluded.

Take eating, for instance. You can start blessing all those who
contributed to bringing your meal to the table. The cook. The
young cashier at the checkout counter of the supermarket. The driv-
ers and transporters who brought the food to the store. All those
who contributed to the packaging of the food—this could include
Canadian lumberjacks or Arabian oil riggers, not to mention the
motley crew of the Panamanian ship that brought the bananas from
Colombia, the Mexican laborers who harvested your California
tomatoes, the Kenyan and Indonesian peasant farmers who produced the coffee, the Israeli botanists who developed integrated pest
management practices to protect the grapefruits, the farmer from
Indiana who grew the wheat for the bread. The chance is that long
before you have finished your meal, you will have cast a web of
blessings that cover the planet and even beyond. (Don't forget the
sun! Blessing nature in its manifold manifestations and gifts is an
essential part of blessing. For instance, as a great lover of real, craft-
produced honey, I regularly bless bees whose existence is at serious
risk in a growing number of regions due to chemical pollution and
other attacks.)

And blessing your meal and those who helped produce it
might even get you thinking and concerned about the working
conditions of those who produced it. Once you start blessing, you
really can't know what might happen! But one thing is certain: It
can only be manifested as good.

So, at the risk of repeating myself, let me stress that the more
we expect good and affirm it as a law governing our lives, the more
it will be manifested in our existence.

That is why it is so important to start every day by blessing it, with a deep feeling of gratitude, because such blessings are the best way of opening the "floodgates of heaven" (as rendered by a French translation of Malachi 3:10) and letting unlimited good fill our lives. The source is infinite. The only limitation is in our inability or fear of accepting unlimited good—with no strings attached! (Even that limitation is only on the level of our belief systems. And the good news is that we are always free to exchange our beliefs for better ones.)

So, why not start your day by affirming gratefully and with a joyful conviction: *Divine Love, acting on the law of attraction throughout the universe, brings into my life exactly what I need to experience, grow, and progress in the present moment and to fill the cup of my joy now.*

Say it thoughtfully. Ponder the words as you say them. Repeat them at various times during the day. And see what happens!

On Your Path to Blessing

How do you normally begin your day?

What kind of blessing could you say to start your day in alignment with the law of positive expectations? Think of all aspects of your day, from work, to family, to friends, to your hobbies.

Try this every morning for a two weeks and observe the effects.

5

THE LAW OF RIGHT RETURNS

*On meeting people and talking to them, bless them in their health,
their work, their joy, their relationship to the universe, themselves,
and others. Bless them in their abundance and their finances,
bless them in every conceivable way, for such blessings not only
sow seeds of healing but one day will spring forth as
flowers in the waste places of your own life.*

The law of right returns has been explained in many ways in the great spiritual teachings of humanity. You may have heard it described as karma, as it is called in many Oriental teachings. It is also called the law of cause and effect: On the spiritual level every cause is seen as having an effect.

🌿 The Koran has a variety of verses making this point; for instance: "And ye will be paid on the Day of resurrection only that which ye have fairly earned" (III, 185).

🌿 The New Testament states clearly, "Whatsoever a man soweth, that shall he also reap" (Galatians 6:7).

In his introduction to the Kabbalah, Rabbi Adin Steinsaltz comments, "Everything that a man does creates in return a vital flux; the totality of his spiritual being is involved in each of his actions."

🌿 Confucian teachings state, "What comes out of you shall return."

🌿 Hinduism reminds seekers, "You cannot harvest what you have not sown. The tree will grow as you sow it."

🌿 We can find this theme throughout the Hebrew scriptures. For instance, Proverbs 14:32 states that "the wicked is driven away in his wickedness."

In the Christian conception of life, grace can annul the law of right returns, or cause and effect, but only if certain conditions are fulfilled, such as sincere repentance. (See chapter 12 for comments on the parable of the Prodigal Son.)

THE POWERFUL EFFECTS OF THOUGHTS

We live in a universe where all is energy. The most modest movement requires an expenditure of energy, but the most powerful energy of all is thought—because it gives birth to all the rest. One might say that on the level of the mind, thoughts are like boomerangs. We need to heed the thoughts we send out into the universe, for sooner or later they will return to us, with increased negative or positive energy.

The teachings of African sage Tierno Bokar, as reported by the Malian philosopher Amadou Hampaté Bâ, illustrate this in a striking metaphor.

Bokar was explaining to a group of his students that the most profitable good deed consisted of praying for one's enemies. In cursing one's foes, said Bokar, one did far more harm to oneself than in blessing them. One of the students said he did not understand this, since a powerful curse, well-aimed, could destroy an enemy. (This needs to be understood in the context of the traditional African system of beliefs, with its frequent reliance on black magic, voodoo, and similar mental practices.)

Bokar answered the student with the parable of the white and black birds:

> In their relations between themselves, men are like two walls facing each other. Each wall is full of small niches in which nest black and white birds. The black birds are our bad thoughts or words. The white birds represent our good thoughts or words. The white birds, because of their shape, can only enter the holes for white birds, and the same is true for the black birds which can only nest in the holes for black birds.

Then Bokar had his student imagine two men who consider themselves enemies, Ali and Youssouf. One day, persuaded that Ali is fomenting evil against him, Youssouf sends him an evil thought, thereby releasing a black bird and freeing a niche of the same color. The black thought-bird of Youssouf flies in the direction of Ali's wall, looking for an unoccupied black niche of its shape. Let us imagine that Ali did not respond by sending a harmful thought (a black bird in the parable). No black niche will be available for Youssouf's oncoming bird, so it will return to its original niche in Youssouf's wall, laden with the evil it carries. Not having managed to harm Ali, it will harm Youssouf—for evil, explained Bokar, never stays inactive, even (and especially) to the one who gives birth to it.

If, on the other hand, Ali plays into the hands of his supposed enemy (for all this is happening on the subjective level of the two men's imaginations) and also sends out a black thought-bird, he will immediately free a black niche into which Youssouf's black bird will enter and deposit part of the evil with which it is loaded. Meanwhile, Ali's negative messenger will have deposited its load of hate into the niche freed by Youssouf's black bird. Thus both black birds will have reached their goal and harmed the people they were aimed at.

"But," added Bokar,

once their task is accomplished, each bird will return to its original nest, for it is said, "Each thing returns to its source." The evil with which they were loaded not being depleted, this evil will turn against its authors and will finish by destroying them. The author of an evil thought, an evil wish, or a curse is thus hurt by both his enemy's black bird and his own black bird when it returns to him.

Of course, the same mechanism functions with the white birds, but positively. If, whatever the circumstances, we send out only good thoughts, only blessings, when our enemy is sending us just the contrary, his black birds will not find a place to rest, and ours will return filled with the positive energy which they carried with them. And the black birds of our opponent will be returned to sender stronger than when they left.

"Thus," concluded Bokar,

if we send out only good thoughts, no evil, no curse can ever reach us in our being. That is why we must always bless friend and foe alike. Not only will the blessing fly toward its objective to fulfill its mission of appeasement, but it will one day or another return to us with all the good with which it was loaded.

UNSELFED LOVE

In Tierno Bokar's explanation, however, we can still discern a residue of self-interest—my good thoughts will return to me and do me good. There is another level of consciousness from which to practice blessing, and that is a state of totally "unselfed" love, where all concern for the human self or ego has simply melted away. It is that state where, to use the beautiful metaphor of the Indian poet Rabindranath Tagore, one's life is turned into a simple reed flute that the divine fills with its own music.

That is why loving unconditionally is the most important activity in the whole universe, and the one most able to produce the deepest happiness. We do not love unconditionally to satisfy some abstract moral law or some faraway deity. As the French writer Antoine de Saint-Exupéry, author of *The Little Prince*, wrote, "You love because you love. There is no reason to love." If the very ground of our being, our very essence, is love—which is one of the postulates of this book—then love is simply the most genuine, the most natural expression of our true being. And in active love, we will also discover a wonderful path toward happiness, health, and fulfillment—but it will be an unintended result, so to speak. As the Koran mentions, "He that does a good deed will be repaid tenfold" (VI, 161).

Love is the very fabric of reality itself. To bless without any expectation of a return, anonymously, is one of the numerous expressions of unconditional love. With time, you will find a sweet joy that is unsurpassed in quietly blessing one and all, from your querulous neighbor to a dictator on the other side of the planet, from the bus driver to the cows that provide such wonderful milk for your table.

In recent years, practitioners of modern medicine have started discovering the astonishing power of love. The well-known American oncologist Dr. Bernie Siegel, in his book *Love, Medicine and Miracles*, explains that modern medicine now has unquestionable proof of the capacity of love to heal and help us stay in good health. Dr. Gerald Jampolsky, author of *Forgiveness* and *Love Is Letting Go of Fear*, says about insanity: "If I were allowed to rewrite the American Psychiatric Association Manual of Diagnoses, it would be one page and it would read: insanity is when we are not experiencing ourselves as love and giving that love away." (He defines sanity as the reverse, i.e., giving love away and experiencing yourself as love.)

To most people, and no doubt many readers of this book, unconditional love may seem very, very far away when we think of the little mean thoughts and deeds that still infiltrate our daily lives. We could become discouraged simply thinking about aiming to live a life of unconditional love! But feeling discouraged would be a mistake.

Sir Philip Sidney, over four hundred years ago, said, "Who shoots at the mid-day sun, though he be sure he shall never hit the mark, yet as sure he is, that he shall shoot higher than he who aims at a bush." Echoing his thought in a few words three centuries later, Ralph Waldo Emerson wrote, "Hitch your wagon to a star." To reach high, we need to start by aiming high.

The experience of a precious friend of mine illustrates what wonderful things can result from unconditional love and blessing without expectation to benefit from it. Her marriage, which had for twenty years been almost daily hell, finally ended in a divorce. Through her trials she had reached a developed spiritual life and was extremely happy in her new activities in the humanitarian field. There was no room in her life for another man, and she felt that the chapter "Relations with the Other Sex" was, on an intimate level, definitively closed.

Then one day, in the course of her work, she met a man involved in the same field of activity as she. Accepting an invitation to have dinner in his apartment on top of a small mountain overlooking a lake, she spent an exceptional evening in his company. They had a deep spiritual exchange.

Driving home, she felt he was the most beautiful human being she had ever met. A rare sense of joy came over her as she thought of the happiness and fulfillment he would one day bring to another woman. She blessed that unknown woman, wishing her all the best in the world.

A few months later, in a mountain site of stunning beauty, her new friend placed a ring on her finger, sealing their togetherness.

An interesting sideline to this story is that this man had been secretly hoping to one day marry a woman who had been very unhappy in her first marriage, so as to enable her to discover a deeper quality of happiness. So on both sides, the secret desire to bless unselfishly enabled a marriage which, still today, many years later, expresses rare freedom and joy.

ALL IS ONE

One of the most powerful states of awareness we can reach on the spiritual level, which is echoed in the writings of many mystics, is that somewhere, at a level of consciousness far deeper than the pedestrian and fleeting material awareness of everyday life, *all is one*. As stated by the Sufi mystic Kabir, "Behold but One in all things. It is the second that leads you astray."

Because all is one, the qualities we claim (or omit to claim) for others, we claim (or omit to claim) for ourselves. At a spiritual level, we see ourselves exactly as we see others. My brother or my sister is the mirror I have of myself.

In a passage of such social radicalism that Karl Marx's *Capital* pales in comparison, the prophet Isaiah (58:6–8) stresses the impossibility of separating our own good from that of our brother or sister—and vice versa. He reminds us that we cannot be whole and healthy, complete, until our neighbor is, too:

Is not this the fast that I have chosen?
To loose the bands of wickedness,
To undo the heavy burdens, and to let the oppressed go free,
And that ye break every yoke?

Is it not to deal thy bread to the hungry,
And that thou bring the poor that are cast out to thy house?
When thou seest the naked, that thou cover him;
And that thou hide not thyself from thine own flesh?

Then shall thy light break forth as the morning,
And thine health shall spring forth speedily.

What is striking in this passage is that the prophet makes a causal link between our wholeness, our healing, and our concern for and actions on behalf of those who are social outcasts—immigrants, refugees, prisoners—and those suffering oppressions of all kind: women working in *maquiladores* in Latin America to make the cheap clothing we are privileged to purchase in our stores; the five-year-old children in Southeast Asia weaving carpets ten to twelve hours a day for our living rooms; the homeless and exploited in our own country and the millions of refugees roaming the world, a majority of them women and children; the two million children who become objects of sexual exploitation worldwide every year—including in our large cities ... the list could continue for pages.

As former South African President Nelson Mandela writes in his powerful autobiography *Long Walk to Freedom*, "Freedom is indivisible; the chains on any one of my people were the chains on all of them, the chains on all my people were the chains on me. ... For to be free is not merely to cast off one's chains, but to live in a way that respects and enhances the freedom of others." Freedom, which is an aspect of wholeness, cannot be a private possession.

As I was preparing this book, I received a letter from a young man named Jacques who was unemployed and living in desperate poverty in Ouagadougou, the capital city of Burkina Faso, West Africa. His words echoed those of Isaiah in an uncanny way.

If you have a brother who is at the other side of the world, and who is suffering great ills of all sorts, and you are there, in good health—although you may appear in good health, you are sick because of your brother who is not in good health but who cannot be separated from you in spirit. Hence you are both sick, because he is linked by the same love.

What Jacques is saying is that we are all one, and that if some think they can live comfortable and rather uncaring lives while others suffer, they are in fact seriously ill, spiritually speaking. Eckhart Tolle has said, "[Loving] your neighbor as yourself means your neighbor is yourself, and that recognition of oneness is love." Replace loving with blessing and you will one day realize that when you bless your neighbor from the bottom of the heart, with utter sincerity, you are also blessing yourself. Because we are all one.

THE LAW OF RIGHT RETURNS IN ACTION

The law of right returns works on all levels of life. Here is a modest example that happened to me when writing the French version of this book. I had just quit my salaried job to become an independent trainer, or coach. It was not easy, at a time when the market was considered depressed, when both private businesses and public administrations were cutting down on training, and when more and more people were starting out as independent trainers—one of the very few professions in my country, Switzerland, for which there was no officially recognized diploma. During the first month of activity, I had practically no income.

One evening, an African friend phoned me to tell me about the plight of a common acquaintance of ours studying in London. This person had not received the scholarship promised to him by his government and was in a desperate financial situation. Could I help, he asked. I explained my situation, saying that for the moment it was impossible for me to do anything, as I myself had almost no income. Later in the evening, I changed my mind and sent him some of the savings I had in the bank.

A few weeks later, I was interviewed on an excellent radio program about a book I had just published and the "Living Simply" workshops I had created. An old friend of my deceased father, whom I had not seen or heard from for at least ten years, heard the talk show and sent me exactly twice the sum I had sent my friend in London. The white bird had returned to nest, accompanied by a generous companion!

On another occasion, I had made a loan to a friend, equivalent to three months' income. We had planned a repayment schedule over two years. At the end of this period he had only repaid about 2 percent. My inner voice told me to forgive 60 percent of the debt. A few days after making this decision, the taxation department of the canton of Geneva, where I live, reimbursed me, quite unexpectedly, a third of the sum I had decided to forgive. I then phoned my friend to inform him of my decision. A few days later, the same department reimbursed me a sum equivalent to the other two-thirds of the sum I had renounced! What was startling to me was the amazing synchronicity of the events, the fact that the repayment by the state had been made at a few days' distance, and that the two sums (what I was remitting and what I received) matched.

Because this law of right returns is a law, we can always count on it. It is not something that may or may not happen—it is impersonal, infinitely tender, and always omni-active—active everywhere in the universe.

It is important to stress that there are no formulas for blessing. It is a joyful attitude of the heart, not a ritual, and sincerity is much more important than a specific form.

As Flying Eagle told Patton Boyle, "You want to learn the truth through my words instead of experiencing it yourself. You can not find the truth through what I tell you. Truth can only be grasped through experience."

PRACTICING THE ART OF BLESSING

Blessing is not something we do to attract good into our life; that would be attempting to manipulate the universe. However, the result will be that you will find more and more harmony pouring into your life. You will acquire greater peace of mind, greater poise. These are the added things of which the Bible speaks—the unintended bonus, if I may say! So let me share with you a few of my experiences in the realm of blessing. The first is that blessing is not an act of will. For instance, it will not help you much if the next time you are angry with someone, you clench your fists in your pocket and with forced concentration say, "I must bless this person. I must bless this person!" To turn blessing into something mechanical, or a pure act of will, is to court failure in advance.

It is also important to be specific when blessing people. Blessing means visualizing the person surrounded by a precise form of good—health, abundance, joy, and so on. It should not be a vague statement like, "I bless all dictators." To bless all criminals as a general category probably has far less healing impact than specifically blessing a murderer presented as a monstrous criminal in your local newspaper.

I usually find it more useful (and more demanding) to silently bless those I see specifically and individually rather than collectively in vague terms. With the practice of blessing, you will develop a real intuition about people and just by looking at them will sense their specific need at that moment. It's very beautiful.

Thus, if someone looks profoundly miserable, you might feel led to bless him in the abundance of his joy, for "the material senses present an inverted image of the ultimate splendor and perfection that only the inner eye beholds." If someone looks angry, you might feel inspired to bless her in her peace and her capacity to forgive. I am accustomed to blessing smokers in their deep inner contentment and satisfaction. For if over the years they are ready to spend tens of thousands of dollars for small cylinders of chemically treated, dried, pressed leaves containing a subtly dosed poison that may well substantially limit their life expectancy, there has to be somewhere a deep feeling of lack that pushes them to perpetuate such a self-destructive habit. (A note for smokers: Bless yourself in your freedom, as well as other smokers you meet.) Of course, this kind of "random" blessing stems from a deep sense of compassion, not judgment.

Imagine you feel the media in your region are doing a poor job of reporting on a certain situation. It will help more to bless them in their truthfulness and honesty than to pester them for their bias. I love blessing our local State of Geneva government in its honesty and spirit of service. This kind of blessing is not time or incident specific, but it is very specific in its aim. It may not exactly reflect the current situation, but it is an expression of your hope.

Start out your practice of blessing with these guidelines in mind. Be experimental. Test different ways of blessing until you feel good about one. And *always* stay open to new inspiration. Eventually, as blessing becomes a natural part of your daily life, you will come to discover a way of blessing that is unique and effective for you.

Blessing People in Their Integrity

One of my favorite blessings is for people, organizations, and businesses in their integrity and their oneness with their divine source.

What can be more beautiful than integrity—in the etymological sense ("unbroken wholeness")? *Integrity* is a beautiful word. It refers to something that expresses its original soundness and uncorrupted essence, a state of not wanting but of uprightness, sincerity, radical truthfulness, ultimately a perfect state of being. Who would not want such a blessing! One day I was writing a note for my wife—who is also one of my greatest teachers on the spiritual path—when the following lines on integrity (which she embodies precisely) just flowed from my pen. I would like to share them, in the hope that it will give you a clearer sense of what it means to bless others in their integrity:

Integrity is a quality of being. It is holding on to that which you know to be your highest sense of truth and vision at all times, whatever the cost. It is resonating with that deepest fiber of your being which urges you to peacefully but firmly hold your ground whatever the supposed prestige of the authority or person opposing you—not out of stubbornness, but prompted by the quiet daring of that inner urge in you which says, "This above all: to thine own self be true."

It means following your highest sense of right at all times, whatever the consequences, however lonely the path, and however loud the jeers and mockery of the crowds and philistines.

Integrity is about "speaking truth to power," as the old Quaker saying goes, when silence would be easier or more advantageous to your interests. It is holding on to the power of truth when everyone around you is accepting compromises or pretending it really doesn't matter. It is standing firm and undaunted when others disappear into the underground shelters of their fears or timidity.

Integrity is yet refusing to water down your inner sense of truthfulness even to satisfy, appease, or gain the approval of a loved one.

Above all, integrity means refusing to cheat yourself, lie to yourself, or abide in the doubtful shadow of half-truths. You can cheat and lie to others and be forgiven. You can slip and fall—and even know defeat—and you will rise again. But when you lie to yourself, who is there to forgive you? After that kind of defeat or fall, who will pick you up? And even if you indulge in this supreme absurdity and ultimate sin of deceiving yourself, will not even your inner strength shirk the companionship of one who is scuttling their own ship? Then only grace can save you.

Deceiving oneself kills the discernment that is the basis of inspired discretion and worthwhile choice. This attitude of consciously eluding what one knows to be true, of lying to oneself is possibly the most harmful attitude anyone can have, because it destroys the soul.

Integrity is a state of being reflecting unbroken wholeness, complete soundness of mind, a quality of sterling authenticity. It carries with it a sense of impeccability, entireness, "of having no part or element taken away or wanting," to quote the Oxford English Dictionary. Integrity is totally genuine, unmarred by compromise, undiluted by approximation, founded in law, always upright because its backbone is Principle.

Integrity tolerates no sloppiness of thought, word, or deed. It demands constant alertness on the part of its followers because it gives them everything—even the keys of the kingdom. Integrity is undisturbed, lucid, totally genuine, flawless, unfeebled by hesitation or doubt. It is sharp, focused, decisive, accurate, precise, and unerring in its direction.

Integrity, as the ultimate core of true being, as the very marrow of our identity, is the foundation and ground of all qualities, starting with love. It is the fabric on which we thread exquisite texture into the tapestry of our existence and achievements. No fabric, no tapestry. When married to love in the joyful dance of one whose existence is a celebration of life, it forms the perfect couple.

Finally, integrity is the twin of spiritual innocence. It is that quality of consciousness that enables you to look every morning into the mirror and say,

"I love what I behold,"
and say to thy brother,
"I saw thy face as the face of God."

It is that pristine purity of being and motive from which spring all great endeavors, all powerful visions, all deep yearnings, all true blessing.

So, when winds and tempests howl, or the tempter whispers, "Compromise," or attempts to make us evade the challenges that we need to face to grow and stay awake, let us hold on, friend, whatever the cost, to that inner fount of true integrity—for it is life itself.

However tough this may be, you will be the ultimate beneficiary, because we always reap what we sow.

BLESSING PEOPLE IN THEIR HAPPINESS

You will also probably experience a very special joy in blessing people in their happiness. For happiness, as noted by the French writer Blaise Pascal, is a state to which all people aspire. In my wanderings through over forty countries of the five continents, I have met only one person who told me happiness was not a concern for him.

As Isaiah 58 stresses, we cannot be totally happy as long as we have the consciousness that others are suffering. The suffering of street children, drug addicts, millions of refugees, and so many other forms of suffering influence all of us deeply, albeit at an unconscious level, because somewhere *we are all one.*

What a wonderful encouragement on the spiritual path to realize that each unselfed blessing we send out will one day bless us and "spring forth as flowers in the waste places of your own life." But once more, this is not the reason for which we bless! You will see that as you bless you will find immense joy, because there is no state of mind happier, more fulfilled than that of the person who rests in a state of perpetual blessing and gratitude.

Another reason it is important to bless is that other people's subconscious often picks up, usually unbeknownst to us or them, the thoughts we entertain about them (and vice versa). These thoughts have an impact on the quality of each relationship. To illustrate, most people know that although journalists who present the TV news give the impression of saying it all by heart, in fact they are reading from a screen in front of them called a teleprompter. We all have an invisible teleprompter, so to speak, on our chest, and others pick up, unconsciously, what we are thinking of them. If we were all aware of this, we would be much more careful about the quality of our thoughts.

Intuitively, we are conscious of this already. For instance, you have certainly been in the presence of a person who said nothing, yet exuded an absolutely wonderful (or maybe terribly unpleasant) energy. Or perhaps you have glanced into the eyes of someone and felt a deep sense of peace. Such experiences are due to the fact that at a deeper level you are conscious of what that person feels for you and for others in general. By blessing people in their happiness, your invisible teleprompter lets others sense the good wishes you have toward them.

WHEN BLESSING ISN'T EASY

To bless people who have harmed you, or with whom you have had difficult relationships, is sometimes anything but an easy exercise! A friend who read this manuscript before publication wrote some comments which are worth sharing:

> I feel that someone who has no experience of self-development or the spiritual life can feel lost, or even guilty, if they don't manage to apply these concepts in their own existence. I know by experience that it is anything but easy to bless one's enemy. One day I decided to bless Rupert, a person at the office, because the situation at work seemed hopeless. Yet blessing him seemed beyond my abilities. That was really going too far!
>
> So I found a way of overcoming this mental block. I blessed him in the perseverance he was showing in teaching me the lessons I needed to learn. And it worked! Afterwards, it enabled me to bless him. But I needed to find an entry, so to speak, that was accessible to me.

So, just like this friend did, *experiment* with the art of blessing. Explore it. Be pragmatic. It behooves us to avoid all ritualism. Blessing is not a magic trick. But if you persevere and let the heart speak, forgiving your own resistances, the fruits will be manifested as certainly as flowers blossom at springtime.

Here is a simple exercise that might help you. Take an unhurried moment, alone in a quiet room or in the countryside. Imagine the people with whom you have real difficulties in life (it could even be political personalities or other public figures). They are all gathered together with one single aim in mind: to bless you. You would certainly be deeply moved, at the very least.

So if you would feel great joy and ease to be blessed by those who create problems for you, why not be the one who takes the initiative of reversing the negative energy by starting to bless them? Instead of feeling the victim of a situation you can't control (or so you believed until now), you would feel suddenly responsible, empowered, active, capable of taking the initiative. You would manifest your dominion, instead of simply submitting to an apparently helpless situation.

Each one of us has, deep down inside, a secret door waiting to be opened and an inner voice ready to guide us, if we give it the space and time to make its presence known.[1]

So, if you feel resistances to blessing someone, settle down alone in a quiet corner. Be sure no one will interrupt you. Take the time needed. Start by relaxing. If need be, put on some restful music, inhale and exhale deeply, stretch a little. Then, turn off the music, and in the ensuing silence, ask: what do I need to learn to have a breakthrough?

You can address the request to the divine being, whoever She may be, to your inner wisdom, or to your inner guide—whatever speaks to you. The important thing is your deep desire to progress, to learn. The reply will certainly come—maybe at a totally unexpected time or in an unexpected manner. But it will come.

Providence, the universe, the infinitely tender and strong fount of unlimited Love cherishes you totally and wants your

happiness more than anything else, more than you could *ever wish
for it yourself.*

Could the plan of a Being of such unconditional goodness ever
be thwarted?

On Your Path to Blessing

*How have you experienced the law of right
returns in your own life?*

*You may have done something positive for
someone that came back to benefit you, or
the opposite—something negative that came
back to hurt you.*

*Can you remember a time when you acted out
of unselfed love, when all concern for yourself melted away?*

What happened and how did you feel?

*Who would you bless in their integrity? Who
in their happiness?*

NOTE

1. The passage on the secret door within refers to *Opening Doors
Within* by Eileen Caddy, one of the founders of the Findhorn Foundation
spiritual community in Scotland. This book, published in many languages, is a favorite with spiritual seekers all around the world. I warmly
recommend it to beginners on the spiritual path—and to more advanced
students too!

6
THE GOLDEN RULE

*As you walk, bless the city in which you live, its government and
teachers, its nurses and street sweepers, its children and bankers, its
priests and prostitutes. The minute anyone expresses the least aggression
or unkindness to you, respond with a blessing. Bless them totally,
sincerely, joyfully—for such blessings are a shield that
protects them from the ignorance of their misdeed
and deflects the arrow that was aimed at you.*

If we expressed aggression, hostility, fear, or lack of kindness
toward someone, would we not prefer them to react with love,
trust, and forgiveness, rather than respond to us in kind? The
reply to this question is so evident that the question itself sounds
rather artificial.

You may be well aware of the Golden Rule, which states,
"Therefore all things whatsoever ye would that men should do to
you, do ye even so to them" (Matthew 7:12)—this is the essence
of all true religion. Is it not fascinating to realize that most of the
great world religions teach exactly the same thing?

🌿 The Islamic Sunna (or tradition) states, "No one of you is
a believer until he desires for his brother that which he
desires for himself" (Sahih Bukhari 2.6.1).

❧ Brahmanism, the orthodox form of Hinduism, says, "This is the sum of duty. Do not unto others that which would cause you pain if done to you" (Mahabarata 5, 1517).

❧ In Judaism, we find the following statement: "What is hateful to you, do not to our fellow man. That is the entire Law, all the rest is commentary" (Talmud, Sabbat 310).

❧ Buddhist practice recommends, "Hurt not others in ways that you find hurtful" (Udana Varga, 5:18).

❧ Confucianism addresses its followers thus: "Surely it is the maxim of loving kindness: do not unto others that which you would not have done unto you" (Analects 15:23).

❧ In Taoism, the Golden Rule is stated as follows: "Regard your neighbor's gain as your gain and your neighbor's losses as your losses" (T'ai Shang Kan Ying Pien).

❧ Zoroastrism, which originated in Persia, upholds, "That nature alone is good which refrains from doing unto another whatsoever is not good for itself" (Dadistan-i-dinik, 94:5).

The impact of the Golden Rule goes still much further when you apply it not only to your behavior but also your thoughts—because your thoughts form the basis for all your words and deeds. This expanded Golden Rule would read: "Think of others exactly in the same way you would want them to think of you." There can be no more demanding and stimulating spiritual discipline than this, no practice that requires more effort and perseverance. And blessing is one of the most privileged paths of getting there!

BLESSING AS ARMOR

Blessing those who attack us in any manner, in word or deed, truly constitutes impenetrable armor and prevents the arrows aimed at us from wounding us inside, even if we are touched physically, for the minute we are clothed with the love such blessings express, we are no longer at the mercy of outside circumstances, people, forces, or events.

A few years ago, I was accompanying an African peasant leader and friend, Demba, to the Geneva train station after he had spent a few days at my home. Just before reaching the station, I noticed a man I had already seen a few weeks before, almost at the same spot. Rarely in my existence had I seen a face expressing such total desolation, eyes so empty and drained of any trace of life. I had spontaneously blessed him then. This time, I was carrying two very heavy suitcases. We passed each other, and for a split second our eyes met. For an instant, I thought, *This poor fellow must be drugged.* Then, as he passed me, he punched me with great force on the mouth and nose and ran off at full speed.

I fell flat out on the pavement, and blood started pouring from my nose. Without a second's hesitation, I started blessing him and encouraged Demba, who was at a total loss, to do the same. We continued to the train track. In less than two minutes, the bleeding had stopped. My friend was the one who needed to be consoled! Back home, I washed my face without even giving a glance at my appearance, including the swollen lip. A few hours later, my wife, Elly, returned home and did not notice a thing.

If I had run after the man, aside from the unpleasant alter-
cation that would certainly have ensued, the hemorrhage would
have been seriously aggravated by the adrenaline pumped into my
system as the result of my anger. The complete calm that filled me,
the feelings of sincere compassion I felt for the man, enabled an
exceptionally rapid healing.

The real victim in this situation was the man who had reacted
violently, certainly without even knowing why he had behaved in
this manner.

Of course, I couldn't help asking myself why this had happened. What was the lesson I was supposed to learn? A few weeks
later, I took a workshop with spiritual teacher Eileen Caddy at the
Findhorn Foundation in Scotland. Possibly the first eco-spiritual
community in the world, Findhorn was founded in the sixties by
Eileen; her husband, Peter Caddy; and Dorothy Maclean. I told her
of the incident, and without a moment's hesitation, she said, "Stop
punching yourself!" At the time, I still indulged in the useless habit
of berating myself, sometimes rather ferociously, for what I considered my shortcomings. Hence the outside event was simply the
translation of an inner state of mind that needed correcting.

What a marvelous place the universe is—when we learn to
read its messages. They do not all come in such an abrupt manner
(thank God!), but they come as we need them and as we are ready
to understand. When the inspiration for the text on *The Gentle
Art of Blessing* came to me sometime before this encounter on the
street, it included the sentence,

When . . . some unexpected event knocks down your plans and
you also, *burst into blessing, for life is teaching you a lesson,
and the very event you believe to be unwanted, you yourself*

called forth, so as to learn the lesson you might balk against were you not to bless it.

This was precisely what had happened at the Geneva train station—and what Eileen was inspired to explain in her own unique manner.

THE GIFT OF SPIRIT LESSONS

Since that incident, I have learned to be much gentler toward myself. I have also learned that with the persistent and stubborn gentleness that characterizes it, life places on our path exactly the kind of experiences appropriate to teaching us the lessons we need to learn at any given moment.

When we begin to learn that constant progression spiritward is a fundamental law of the universe, existence becomes tremendously exciting, because *absolutely every event* can become an opportunity to learn a needed lesson or to discover some powerful new vista. I have at moments the clear vision that my life is programmed for perfection. Life, the universal law of harmony, our divine Mother, infinite Love, will not let go of us until we have learned whatever we need to learn to graduate to a higher level of consciousness, where we will have new lessons. It may well have been an insight of this kind into the incredibly beautiful, considerate, loving functioning of the law of constant progression that enabled Paul to claim that he gloried in tribulations and prompted the apostle James to state, "When all kinds of trials and temptations crowd into your lives my brothers, don't resent them as intruders, but welcome them as friends!" (James 1:2, J. B. Phillips translation).

Immediately after my train station experience, I felt something precious had come my way. It was first and foremost a gift of grace, for the strength I discovered had nothing to do with the little human ego making big efforts to control itself. You could say I felt almost like an observer of what was happening. It brought to mind a passage from the commentary of the Hindu holy scripture, the Bhagavad Gita, by the great Indian spiritual master Sri Aurobindo. When our actions repose on the Brahman (the Godhead), he writes, "The personality of the instrumental doer ceases; though he acts, he does nothing; for he has given up not only the fruits of his works, but the works themselves and the doing of them to the Lord." In other words, at a certain level of understanding, we become aware of the fact that the supreme being becomes the Creator, the acts, and the results all at the same time.

Practiced in this spirit, in which we become "an impersonal instrument of the Master of works," as Aurobindo writes elsewhere in the same commentary, the art of blessing takes on a totally new dimension, as we will see in chapter 13. Blessing means to become the music of love, sending serene and silent strains throughout the turbulent atmosphere of our times—which so many of our contemporaries experience as full of anguish and stress.

THE GOLDEN RULE IN ACTION

The most amazing application of the Golden Rule I have ever come across is in the book by Dr. George G. Ritchie, *Return from Tomorrow*. Ritchie was a doctor with the American troops in World War II. He took part in the liberation of the Holocaust victims in the infamous concentration camps of Nazi Germany, where these victims and many others were kept in subhuman conditions.

Ritchie explains that he became acquainted with a Polish prisoner in a camp near Wuppertal. The man was a lawyer with an "unpronounceable name" nicknamed "Wild Bill Cody" by American soldiers because of his long, drooping handlebar mustache. Because Wild Bill radiated health—shining bright eyes, an erect posture, boundless energy—Ritchie assumed he had been brought to the camp shortly before liberation. Fluent in a number of European languages, Wild Bill became an unofficial camp translator, helping the Americans in their numerous tasks. Despite fifteen- and sixteen-hour days with a staggering workload, he never showed any signs of weariness. His compassion for the other inmates was endless. Every ethnic group in the camp—between whom there were numerous hate-filled antagonisms—looked upon him as a friend.

So Ritchie was dumbfounded the day he learned that the Polish lawyer had been in the camp since 1939! He was a medical miracle—totally unexplainable in medical terms, at least at that time. For six years he had lived in disease-ridden barracks, eating unidentifiable "food," surviving in conditions under which thousands of others had either died or been reduced to skeletal vestiges of humanity. Yet there he was, in glowing health, without any sign of mental or even physical deterioration. What was his secret?

One day, over a cup of tea, Wild Bill told Ritchie his story.

At the beginning of the war, he had been living in the Warsaw ghetto with his wife and five children. One day, the Nazis arrived on their street, lined everyone against the wall—except the lawyer, because he spoke German—and opened fire with machine guns, killing everyone, his wife and five children included. Right in front of his eyes. In vain, Wild Bill pleaded to be shot with his family.

He paused, perhaps seeing again his wife and five children. "I had to decide right then," he continued, "whether to let myself hate the soldiers who had done this. It was an easy decision, really. I was a lawyer. In my practice, I had seen too often what hate could do to people's minds and bodies. Hate had just killed the six people who mattered most to me in the world. I decided then that I would spend the rest of my life—whether it was a few days or many years—loving every person I came in contact with."

An interesting point in this amazing story is that the lawyer's decision to forgive and love was not made on religious grounds, in the traditional sense of the word, not as a reply to some religious command or ethical imperative. It was based simply on his observation of life and on the understanding that love regenerates while hate destroys—starting with the one who does the hating.

Today, the relatively new medical discipline of psychoneuroimmunology (PNI—a specialty that studies the relationships of the body, nervous system, and psyche) has revealed that expressing love strengthens the body's immune system. In *Love, Medicine and Miracles*, author Bernie Siegel has disseminated this vital insight to a broad public. We are beginning to see more and more the positive, physical consequences of living love instead of hate, and living in alignment with the golden rule. We follow this rule not because we have to be moral but because it is the ultimate source of our happiness.

THE TRANSFORMING HAND OF LOVE

Returning to the opening quote of this chapter, why would we want to protect aggressors from "the ignorance of their misdeeds"?

Shouldn't they suffer, especially as suffering is often the opportunity for learning much-needed lessons?

Even if that is the case, who among us would not prefer to be transformed by the hand of love, of which blessings are the expression, rather than undergo purification by suffering? Those who do wrong amass far greater anger and negativity against themselves than against others. They harm themselves by hardening themselves and simply delay the day when they will *have* to transcend their malicious or evil thoughts and actions. (Once more, we are programmed for perfection, whether we are aware of it or not.) No one who is of a sound mind could possibly wish suffering or punishment for another. And if the Golden Rule can enable us to help someone avoid suffering—for example, through the grace of silent blessings—would anyone not wish to use such a wonderful gift and the free opportunity to forward "inevitable grace" (to borrow William Wordsworth's powerful expression)?

But, one might object, what about those who consciously plan evil? Not the mentally disturbed person who murders a neighbor in an alcoholic fit in which he has abdicated all self-control, but the respected businessman who uses corruption to gain new markets or the weapons trader who becomes wealthy from selling antipersonnel mines while his government feigns ignorance?

We can learn to bless them in their integrity, which is the very quality they most need to express and seem to lack, because evil is sometimes the highest idea of good some people have. For instance, many young soldiers who are trained to kill believe this is the right way to defend their country. *Each one is at each moment at his or her highest level of consciousness.* This key insight is one of the most powerful tools around to liberate us from judging others. For instance, the highest sense of right for a sports champion—who is aware that the stimulants he is taking are illegal—may be that winning at all costs is the most important pursuit. It represents his ultimate value. At the same time, we need to denounce the evil action in itself, following the old theological distinction: condemn the sin, not the sinner.

No real good can ever be achieved at the cost of another human being. However, even the weapons trader, the dictator, or the person dealing in child pornography has a vision of the universe that makes him erroneously *believe* that he can win at the cost of others losing. If he had a more progressive vision of things, he would rapidly abandon his aggressive behavior. Think of your own life:

Have you ever consciously perpetrated evil, knowing that it was self-destructive as well as harmful to others and persevered in your stance despite the realization that in the long run it was a dead-end road?

At some level, evil is always the result of ignorance, deep confusion, or an inability to see:

🕊 ignorance of the spiritual laws governing the universe, which transcend all other laws

🕊 ignorance that the path of unconditional love, of obedience to the Golden Rule, is the ultimate path to happiness, fulfillment, and freedom for all

🕊 ignorance of the fact that sooner or later the harm we do returns to us—frequently with compounded interest

When confronted with evil of this nature, practicing the Golden Rule through the art of blessing is the most powerful course of action. As a friend once told me,

At the bottom of the worst criminal hides a daughter or son of the Creator ignorant of their divine origin. Only love enables a person who feels at fault, or on the contrary, who is totally convinced of the rightness of their position, to change it. When one is on the defensive, it is very difficult to modify one's point of view, for one only thinks in terms of survival—be it the survival of the little ego or some material privilege.

During the long agony of Zimbabwe in 2008–9, when world media were excoriating President Mugabe, who seemed to have literally lost his mind at the cost of untold suffering to his fellow citizens, this friend spent long moments blessing him. As he asked me, how could Mugabe possibly change, with this wall of hatred surrounding him?

Such an attitude is not only right, it is efficient! It transforms. This is illustrated by a striking story I read a few years ago in the French edition of *The Herald of Christian Science*, a magazine devoted to spiritual healing. The author, a woman, was walking behind two men in the street. The first man entered a store, and as he walked in, unbeknownst to him, his wallet fell from his pocket. The second man rushed over, picked the wallet up and examined it, put it into his pocket—and continued his path.

The author says that instead of mentally condemning this person, she silently and vigorously affirmed the spiritual integrity of man made in God's image. She declared that "the children of God are honest and that the testimony of the senses is a lie: God's child cannot behave incorrectly." Although her eyes showed her a thief, she affirmed that, deep down, this person's authentic spiritual identity was one with its divine source.

Suddenly, the man who had entered the shop and lost his wallet came running out, looking for it everywhere. At that moment, the man who had pocketed it retraced his footsteps, handed the wallet to its rightful owner and, pointing toward the woman who had been affirming spiritual truths silently, said, "This woman told me to return it to you." *Yet the woman had not at any time spoken to him!*

But let us listen to what the woman concerned had to say about the reality hidden behind the appearances:

> *It was his own reaction to the divine Truth which had changed this man's heart. It is important not to entertain negative thoughts about one's neighbor. . . . To love one's neighbor means to acknowledge God's perfect creation in each individual.*

THE SUBJECTIVE NATURE OF EXPERIENCE

This truly amazing story stresses that, behind the façade of material appearances, we inhabit a universe where the mental and spiritual are possibly infinitely more important than we imagine, where people feel and react to our most intimate thoughts, often without either them or us being conscious of it. The awareness of this fact can be very powerful. Jesus mentions it on various occasions, especially when he denounces mental assassination (Matthew 5:21–26). It reinforces the hypothesis that others are subconsciously capable of reading our secret thoughts.

A metaphor will enable us to understand the concept of two simultaneously existing levels of reality or consciousness: the material level, where evil often seems to be happening, and a spiritual level, where a totally different, perfectly harmonious reality reigns. You may have had the experience of taking off in a plane in bad weather. On the ground, it is raining and may be foggy and dark. The plane takes off, rises—and suddenly, you are above the clouds in the most brilliant sunshine with a bright blue sky. You have simply changed levels.

It is the same in everyday life. For a given person, a specific situation reflects the image of discordance, whereas another person will have a completely different awareness of the same situation. As astrophysicist Hubert Reeves once said, tongue in cheek, "Reality has its own ways of surprising us on all sides." Many studies on perception point to the fact that we see what we believe as often as the contrary!

No one can be our enemy (or a total bore, or a pain in the neck, or whatever unflattering names we all occasionally feel like applying to others) unless we ourselves stick such a label upon them. Ultimately, no outside event, encounter, or person can harm us unless we give it the power to do so. This is because all of life is a subjective process of interpretation and definition. Absolutely everything that happens to us in life, everything we are aware of, is filtered through our consciousness, our perception. An event—in itself—does not exist. We interpret all events, all encounters, every single sensual impression. You might say that in this way each person creates his or her own reality, every day, at every single moment.

An American friend gave me a striking example of the fundamentally subjective nature of all experience. This story illustrates how a simple declaration of truth, maintained with absolute conviction, can transform an extreme and apparently hopeless situation, while at the same time blessing the aggressor.

One of her friends, an attractive, young blonde whose figure did not pass unnoticed, decided some years ago to cross Central Park in New York at midnight—not something any sane woman (or man, for that matter) would normally attempt. But this young woman, a devout Christian, had the faith that moves mountains, and especially saw in each person a child of the Creator, whatever the outward appearances might claim to the contrary.

At one moment, the inevitable took place. A man pounced on her from behind a bush where he was lurking, threw her violently to the ground and started tearing at her clothes with evident intentions. Pinned under her aggressor, the young woman repeated slowly, with complete poise, "You are a son of God." Completely dumbfounded, the man just picked himself up and walked away muttering. I wonder what he might have been saying to himself?

This young woman had possibly never heard of the art of blessing. But to disarm a potential rapist with a simple declaration of truth certainly constitutes one of the most powerful and efficient blessings I have ever heard.

What if unconditional love were the *normal* and *rational* response of those who have really grasped the idea that the universe and the self is—not *are*—one? If all is the infinite expression of infinite Love, as certain texts of the mystical literature of all times stress, there can be no division anywhere, no separation, only "unbroken wholeness," to use the beautiful words of physicist David Bohm.

But to live that in everyday life is something else!

On Your Path to Blessing

Think of a notorious evildoer alive today and
try blessing this person.

Think of someone you don't get along with or who has hurt you and try blessing this person.

How could you live the Golden Rule more fully in your everyday life?

7

THE LAW OF
UNCONDITIONAL LOVE

*To bless all without distinction is the ultimate form of giving,
because those you bless will never know from whence came
the sudden ray that burst through the clouds of their skies,
and you will rarely be a witness to the sunlight in their lives....
It is impossible to bless and judge at the same time.*

For the past thirty years, I have spent part of each summer in a
small chalet in the Swiss Alps. The chalet is nestled at close to
seven thousand feet in a hamlet surrounded by an extraordinary
carpet of Alpine flowers. These flowers, especially the bright clus-
ters dancing around the chalet, have taught me important lessons
about the art of blessing. They give indiscriminately to any and
all passersby. Whether you are a saint or a sinner, a millionaire or
a tramp, they offer you their beauty and their perfume freely and
with equal generosity. Their giving knows nothing of vacations or
days off. In sunshine, snow, or rain, they are faithful to their
post—giving, giving, giving unceasingly. Their sharing is natural
and effortless, expressing the essence of their being, which is to
give freely.

Do we have to make efforts to be American or South African, Japanese or Syrian if we are a citizen of one of these countries? Do we wake up in the morning, thinking, "Oh, today, I must really make a big effort to be American (or Japanese)"? No, it is the most effortless thing in the world. We know without any doubt that we are citizens of a given country. In the same way, the day we understand that the depth of our most authentic being is total love, we will start loving and blessing in the same manner the flowers give of their beauty and perfume—effortlessly, naturally. ("Love, which created me, is what I am," states *A Course in Miracles*—can there be a more powerful, liberating, and exciting awareness?) Above all, we will bless unselfconsciously. As Lebanese poet Kahlil Gibran says in *The Prophet*,

There are those who give and know not pain in giving,
nor do they seek joy, nor give with
mindfulness of virtue;

They give as in yonder valley the myrtle breathes
its fragrance into space.

Through the hands of such as these God speaks,
and from behind their eyes He smiles upon the earth.

A life filled with the perfume of such constant unselfconscious blessing can only exude happiness and in itself be a blessing to all those who encounter it. In this respect, I composed a little prayer which I pray many times a day, that goes, "Shine as me, and may I be so Thee that all those I encounter may experience me as Thy radiant presence, Thy unconditional love. May they no longer see me, but only, only, only Thee."

KNOW NOT RESENTMENT OR ANGER

The gift the flowers make to all is also nonviolent. Alpine flowers are usually amazingly resistant—they have to be to survive in such a rugged climate. Walk on them, trample on them—after a moment's astonishment, they will lift their gentle smiling faces, smooth their ruffled petals, as if to say, "My perfume is free. I know neither resentment nor anger."

So why impoverish ourselves by withholding our blessings and measuring with a thimble the love thus expressed? Why delay the moment we will one day all reach—be it here on earth or in a more evolved state of consciousness later on? An awareness resulting in a constant state of blessing and rejoicing, because it acknowledges the divine everywhere. Why stifle our own happiness? Why delay our own entry into the kingdom of joy?

The more we learn to bless unconditionally, the less we judge. It is an amazing inner experience. We simply let others be. In any way, who are we to judge? "Do not judge your neighbor until you walk two moons in his moccasins," says a North American Indian proverb. Let us learn to see in our neighbor the light, rather than the lampshade, adds Dr. Gerald Jampolsky.

Who of us can walk, be it but a few moments, in our neighbor's moccasins? Can I really adopt another's way of thinking, the beliefs someone holds about him or herself and the world, his or her heredity, fears, hopes, the complex fabric of this person's life experiences? For me, this has been one of the greatest benefits of the art of blessing: seeing my frequent, pathetic, trivial judgments slowly fade and shrivel—although I still have a long path to tread before reaching complete nonjudgment!

Some years ago, during a wedding ceremony, I had a sudden, powerful insight into what it would mean to have a mind totally free from all judgment. It was a pure gift of grace, because I don't recollect doing or even thinking anything to have made it come my way. I count this experience as one of the most treasured moments of my existence. The incredible freedom, the inner lightness of being, and the sparkle of a mind no longer tangled in the quagmire of inner criticism, no longer bound by the puny, pitiful habit of weighing life and people on the mean and sad little scale of one-sided judgments. What a state of grace!

This experience left me with a deep longing, since there are few things I wish more ardently than to be freed from all judgment. And I can imagine that what Hindus call a state of Samadhi, or Buddhists Nirvana, or Christians the kingdom of heaven, is a state of consciousness freed from all judgment, because it is aware of good alone and consciously accepts all creatures in their true divine essence.

NONJUDGMENT AND UNCONDITIONAL LOVE

After a life of carefully observing human behavior in many cultures, I have come to the conclusion that a spirit of judgment (with its derivations of labeling, cheap criticism, and above all the habit of comparing people and their achievements) represents *the* social evil *par excellence*. Judgment entertains fear in all areas, kills spontaneity and creativity, crushes joy in its claws, feeds gossip and the spreading of murderous tidbits of personal opinion, poisons hearts and minds, sows doubt.

better or more than all others of the same kind

If you ever, even for a few days, had the opportunity to live with others in an atmosphere devoid of all criticism and judgment, where you were accepted unconditionally just as you are, with your strengths and weaknesses, you are aware of what an extraordinary experience this is. Creativity, joy, and spontaneity burst forth, hearts open, trust and self-confidence blossom.

The expression of unconditional love, including the art of blessing, constitutes the most fundamental force for and affirmation of life. As Flying Eagle says to his friend Patton Boyle, "Love is on a deeper level than feelings. You can not always detect it with your feelings. . . . Love is a dimension like time or space."

Many great spiritual seers agree in teaching the primacy of love. Let us repeat Jesus's statement, "He that doeth truth cometh to the light" (John 3:21). For Jesus, it seems that *doing* the truth consisted first and foremost in *living* love: in relieving suffering, healing disease, showing the way of the fullness of life, and blessing all those he met, everywhere.

Love is possibly the only thing in the universe that is at the same time its own cause, means, and end.

The law of unconditional love assures us that, however difficult the challenge, if we persevere, we shall always win. The victory may not take the form we expected or hoped for, but it will in some way further our progress. However, to be honest, I must say that although I can see this clearly, I am still very much in the early stages of its practice!

To understand this, consider a mother's love for her child. She takes care of the child out of love (this equals love as a cause), she cares for him or her with infinite tenderness (love as a means), and she does all this with no other aim or goal than love (love as an end). Love needs no justification of any sort. It simply is.

There are no neutral thoughts. Every single thought is charged with a certain quality of energy. And, when charged with love, every thought can contribute to the healing of the planet and the transformation of the world. In a period of history where so many people feel powerless to influence world events, is that not an astonishing and most heartening realization? Irish philosopher Edmund Burke noted two centuries ago that the greatest mistake was to do nothing, alleging as a pretext we could only do a little. Or as my favorite Arabic proverb has it, "The person who really wants to do something finds a way, the other person finds an excuse!"

Each of us, by the quality of our thoughts, can become an agent of transformation to the world.

In a little poem published shortly after his death in 1997, Joe Dominguez, coauthor with Vicki Robin of the bestseller *Your Money or Your Life*, wrote,

> *Your natural state is*
> *the ecstatic experience of Love.*
> *It is simply the conscious experience*
> *of our aliveness, made manifest . . . shared.*
>
> *Love does not "happen" to us.*
> *We happen it.*
> *We happen it by removing that which blocks it.*
>
> *Living a life is simply the process of removing*
> *those barriers to experiencing Love.*[1]

The law of unconditional love is perhaps the most fundamental of the spiritual laws. As humankind learns to live according to this law, it turns out to be the very structure or ultimate substance of reality itself. Flying Eagle summarizes the vision of the greatest mystics and seers of humanity when he says to Patton Boyle, "Love is the basic element behind all that is.... It is the elemental essence of the universe."

STRIVING TOWARD UNCONDITIONAL LOVE

A heart full of blessings is like the inner garden of the Sufi mystics. Each person wishes to be permanently in this state! Such a blessing-filled heart *is* possible, on the condition you strive with all your heart and make this goal your deepest desire.

This is explained in the beautiful book by Piero Ferrucci, *Inevitable Grace: Breakthroughs in the Lives of Great Men and Women.* Ferrucci tells the story of an Indian disciple who asks his master what is needed to reach true realization. Rather than give a long explanation, the master pushes his student's head into a lake and holds him there until the disciple struggles to surface.

The master then asks him what he longed for when his head was underwater. "To breathe," answers the disciple. "And how intensely?" asks the master. "With all my strength," replies the disciple. The master says, "When you will feel the same desire to reach the divine, you will be on the right track."

In life, we usually attain what we *really* desire. To desire intensely or not, that is the question, to rephrase Hamlet. Those who are *totally* committed to a goal are giving out a powerful message to the universe. They unconsciously lock themselves into the universal warp of synchronicity. Things start moving. Totally unexpected events begin to unfold. We discover that the universe—infinite, unconditional Love behind the veil of material appearances—is on our side. Or, as Einstein would have said, the universe is friendly. It is exceedingly friendly and utterly loving toward those who live according to its laws. This book is about some of these patterns of synchronicity.

But it is also true that none of this will happen in just one day! Contrary to our materialistic society, which offers instant gratification in almost every field, there are few instant results on the spiritual path, where one of the fundamental qualities demanded is perseverance. Even experiences such as the instant healing of disease or a spiritual epiphany are usually the result of a long inner maturing that suddenly bursts forth like Asian bamboo, which prepares its seed for seven years underground and then grows so vigorously that you can practically measure its growth from one hour to the next.

It took me years of daily blessing until I finally shook off the last traces of resentment toward the people who had forced me to resign—but what a fabulous harvest I made on the way! Today, I can say with utter sincerity how grateful I am the liberation did not happen rapidly, because the lessons learned on the way were both precious and much needed.

Psalms 18:32 says, "'Tis God [infinite Love] that girdeth me with strength and maketh my way perfect." Every day, I see with greater clarity that my way is completely perfect, down to the very smallest detail—and the more I understand this, the more everything in life, down to the smallest detail, acquires meaning. If you become frustrated in your struggle to replace judgment with love, don't despair: The important thing is to continue striving for it and to learn from the lessons the path reveals to you. (We'll discuss this in greater detail in the next chapter.)

LOVING THROUGH BLESSING

The art of blessing is one of the numerous forms which love takes, in a way that is easily accessible to every single person. Everyone can understand and practice it, from people who may be totally illiterate to others with no prior spiritual experience of any sort, even agnostics. Truly, it is one of the most democratic, simple, grassroots forms of spiritual practice that exists, one that is easy to practice (in the sense of not being complicated). Just open your heart and let the blessings flow.

Finally, last but not least, it is a form of love that blesses the person who practices it as much as it does the person who receives it.

The art of blessing is a wonderful opportunity to express the infinite creativity we all reflect as expressions of the Creator. Invent opportunities to bless. You might even create a simple ceremony of your own, be it with your partner, family, friends, on the occasion of a departure or return, whatever—the opportunities to bless are infinite. An hour before writing this paragraph, I accompanied my wife, Elly, to the airport, and she asked me for the first time to bless her before leaving. I was deeply moved, because in her very being she is a daily blessing in my life in so many ways.

A few years ago, after having finished the French version of this book at the little chalet—called Singing Silence—high up in the Swiss Alps where I spend part of my summers every year, I worked very hard for a week enlarging a terrace that faces breathtakingly beautiful mountain scenery. Numerous participants of my "Recreating Your Life" workshops have, over the years, passed unforgettable moments at this spot. But the terrace was rather narrow for a dozen people, so a friend and I moved, by hand, at least two tons of rocks and stones, some of which needed to be carried on an old rucksack frame from far away.

Once the work was finished, I spent a few quiet moments on the terrace, remembering the wonderful moments spent there by visitors whose passages are immortalized in the guest book, which echoes with names from all around the world. Alphabets I cannot decipher leave messages in tongues I may never speak from people I've sometimes never even met. Poets and a Philippine freedom fighter, peasants from the heart of Africa or South America, renowned scientists, housewives, teachers and their classes, Swiss farmers and a Sri Lankan mother, bankers and philosophers, healers and businesspeople. All have left kind words of appreciation and love. An American writer left a few words close to the Wolof annotations of a Senegalese organizer of fisherman's cooperatives, a Kurdish refugee child's signature neighbors that of a world special-ist of insect flight, and Sanskrit rubs shoulders (or rather characters) with French, Dutch with Arabic, and long German words bump (*Ach, Entschuldigung!*) into a brief Italian exclamation.

I blessed all the people who would meet there in the years to come—blessing them in their fullness, their search for meaning, their deep happiness and complete integrity (my favorite blessing). And I was suddenly overwhelmed by an extraordinary feeling of peace and serenity which, I believe, will return every time I tune in to the energy of that magical spot. It is as if, by that simple blessing, I had united myself, on a spiritual level, to all the people who had been at Singing Silence and all those who were still to come there for rest, rejoicing, and healing.

In one of the most meaningful books I have ever read, *A Thou-sand Names for Joy: Living in Harmony with the Way Things Are*, Byron Katie stresses time and time again the superficial nature of most human thinking. For Katie, as most people call her, believing our thoughts is the main cause of suffering. She states that thoughts are no more individual than the television programs we watch! "Thoughts can't ever be a problem to me because I have questioned them and seen that no thought is true.... You either believe in your thoughts or you don't; there's no other choice," she writes.

I have started visualizing and yearning for the day when I shall discard all these useless thoughts that seem to cram into the waiting room of my mind and replace them with simple blessings. That will be coming back to essentials; that will be lifting the veil and seeing more of the true nature of things. Join me there!

On Your Path to Blessing

Have you ever been in the presence of someone who loves you unconditionally? How did it make you feel?

Think of the people you judge on a daily basis. How would it feel to replace judgment with acceptance?

How can you practice unconditional love in your life?

NOTE

1. The poem was published in F.I. News and Notes, September 1997, a newsletter of the New Road Map Foundation, P.O. Box 15981, Seattle, WA 98115. This foundation does pioneering work helping people handle money in a more responsible and joyful way, to lead to more fulfilled, uncluttered lives—the latter being essential to anyone who wishes to progress spiritually.

8

THE LAW OF UNIVERSAL HARMONY

When something goes completely askew in your day,
when some unexpected event upsets your plans—and you—
burst into blessing. For life is teaching you a lesson, and the very
event you believe to be unwanted, you yourself called forth,
so as to learn the lesson you might balk against were you
not to bless it. Trials are blessings in disguise,
and hosts of angels follow in their path.

Practicing blessing showed me that this gentle art is intrinsically linked to another spiritual truth: a fundamental law of harmony governs all beings in order to guide and adjust all things for our good.

This law reflects the infinite Love that governs the universe. We experience the support and guidance of this law on condition that we live according to our highest sense of what is right and true.

More and more frequently, contemporary literature on personal and spiritual development mentions the idea that the universe is a sort of pedagogical laboratory, or a school if you prefer. We are here to learn the spiritual laws governing the universe. The more we live our lives according to these laws, the more our lives will reflect greater fullness, harmony, joy, peace, and contentment.

By definition, a universal law is something that applies to all situations and circumstances, everywhere, for everyone, in a completely impersonal manner. The laws governing the growth of roses function in the same manner for a French gardener with blond hair or a Turkish gardener with dark hair. A rose wouldn't think, "Well, I confess to having a weak spot for French gardeners, especially blond ones with mustaches like Henri, so I will grow a little faster and make myself a little more attractive."

Therefore, there is no situation, person, or circumstance that could in any way be outside the reach and protection of this law, because it is also infinite. There is no person who could be too bad, insignificant, immoral, worthless, or just plain uninteresting not to be supported by the firm yet infinitely tender care of this Love operating as law in every nook and cranny of the universe.

If this is so—and this is the vision of some of the great spiritual teachings of humanity—then each challenge, difficulty, and trial conceals a secret gift, a hidden blessing that can contribute to our growth toward greater fulfillment—even trials that might appear totally destructive (for example, the earlier story of the Jewish lawyer from the Warsaw ghetto, or see chapter 11 for the nonviolent disarming of a band of murderers by spiritual power alone). The apostle Paul expressed this universal truth in his own words when he stated, "All things work together for good for them that love God" (Romans 8:28).

J. B. Phillips translates this: "Moreover we know that to those who love God ... everything that happens fits into a pattern for good" (Romans 8:28). *All* things—not most things all the time, or some things all the time, or everything for everyone except me. There is no exception to a law. When you put a kettle on the stove, you don't hope it's going to boil. You don't tell your guests,

"If the laws of thermodynamics are working today, we should hopefully have a cup of tea in ten minutes." You say, "Tea will be ready in a jiffy. Just relax and make yourselves at home."

In the omnipresence of the law of infinite, unconditional Love, we can relax, because we *are* at home. Everywhere. Whatever the material appearances may scream to the contrary—and in today's world, they are admittedly screaming rather loudly!

To suggest that we ourselves call forth certain situations in our lives—including some rather unpleasant or difficult ones—sounds rather provocative. But have you not noticed in your environment people who repeatedly put themselves in the same situations? A woman friend who constantly ends up with violent men who beat her? A person who repeatedly has accidents, or who loses keys or a purse time and time again? Someone who never gets along with his superiors or colleagues at work? Or on the other hand, the fortunate ones who succeed in everything they do? The friend who has the perfect husband and delightful children who are all performing brilliantly in school, who is never sick, and whose petunias are always the most beautiful in the neighborhood?

It seems as if, somewhere, in some strange way, we program ourselves to be in certain situations where we are going to have to learn certain lessons. And we will repeat the situations until the lesson is learned.

When I was a youngster, I was always having sinus trouble. One day a kindly nose and throat specialist solemnly proclaimed to my mother and me that I caught sinusitis because I went bareheaded in the rain. I would always, he certified with the great authority with which we endowed him, catch sinusitis if I walked bare-headed in the rain. And of course I did. It worked. Each time!

Yes, it worked with great reliability—until I understood that my body was an incredible invention, superbly programmed to faithfully fulfill all the beliefs I held about it. The doctor's statement was not even remotely scientific. It was an educated belief I had accepted. (After all, there were so many diplomas on the wall of his office!) One day I simply decided to no longer accept it. I decided I would enjoy the wondrous freedom of walking "bearheaded" in the rain (i.e., like bears—wearing no hat). I thought that rain, which was such a precious gift of Divinity, was certainly not programmed to produce sinusitis. And of course, I haven't had sinusitis for over fifty years, despite the fact that I have been cycling in all climes, summer and winter, usually without a hat, for all that time.

The idea that in some way we are programming our lives—or at least calling forth the events needed to further our growth—is tremendously challenging and certainly raises as many questions as it does answers. However, it is also immensely liberating if we can accept the idea of a fundamental law of harmony governing the universe—which, admittedly, is a great act of faith, although it requires far less faith than believing the universe is run by chance! When asked what the most important question concerning the future of the human race is, the great scientist Albert Einstein replied, "Is the universe friendly?"

Dear reader, I believe the universe is not only friendly, but is a place that functions with such delicate intricacy, such superb synchronicity, such a harmonious pattern of interrelatedness, such utter perfection, that it so gently and tenderly takes care of every one of its creatures, that we would be utterly speechless if we could but for a few seconds catch a glimpse of it all. Even past suffering, in this context, can be redeemed and be blessed.

BLESSINGS IN RETROSPECT

A friend shared with me how a great suffering in his childhood, which at the time seemed totally useless and negative and absolutely unredeemable, was later in his life turned into something positive.

He had been brought up in a religious environment where sex was practically taboo. All the innuendos, hints, and unspoken attitudes around him suggested that it was something very sinful, albeit incredibly attractive. The rationale tormented him. How could God make something at the same time so desirable and so sinful? It seemed almost sadistic. So he repressed his adolescent urges the best he could: he took cold baths, lay naked on the wooden floor, even scourged himself. This resulted in an array of psychosomatic disorders. It was only many years later that, having left the stern religion of his childhood and struggled to find a new balance in life, he discovered peace in this area of his existence.

Later in his career, my friend was called upon to introduce sex education to adolescents of the Muslim country where he lived. He was surprised to find himself face-to-face with repressive puritan attitudes reminiscent of what he had known in his own childhood, with all the attendant psychological misery. He had contacts with young people of both sexes who were absolutely desperate, sometimes threatening suicide, so dire were their seemingly intractable problems. "Often, it is only because of the immense suffering I myself had gone through in this area that I was able to understand

and empathize deeply with these young people," he told me. "It stretched my listening and gave me a compassion I would certainly never have felt had I had a normal adolescence in this area." He then quoted the striking statement of the prophet Joel (2:25), who wrote, "I will restore to you the years that the locust hath eaten."

In other words, we can transform our past by transforming our consciousness about the past—for the simple reason that the past only exists in our present thinking about past events. We re-create our past by the thoughts we hold about it in the present. When, time and time again, we go over events of the past in our mind, sometimes dozens or even hundreds of times, we are digging an ever deeper groove, so to speak, from which it can be increasingly difficult to escape. So it is important to realize we can very literally re-create our past by changing our thoughts and feelings about it. In the case of my friend, what had seemed a hopelessly useless negative experience became a springboard toward deeper compassion.

We can always start anew. Even if we have failed a thousand times, we can succeed the 1001st time. Specialists of the Bible have estimated that the paralyzed man at the pool of Bethesda, whom Jesus healed instantaneously after thirty-eight years of illness, had attempted to reach the supposedly miraculous pool more than fourteen thousand times!

Can you imagine all the self-programmed expectations of failure that this person must have entertained (while at the same time harboring deep down at least a glimmer of hope)? Christian Science founder Mary Baker Eddy once wrote, "Tireless Being, patient of man's procrastination, affords him fresh opportunities every hour." What a remarkable statement. However discouraged we may feel, however apparently hopeless the situation, infinite Love waits patiently at the door of our consciousness. It will never desert its post. It will never, ever leave. It cannot ever become impatient with the waiting, for it has eternity on its side.

By the time my friend took on the task of providing sex education, he had forgiven those who had instilled limited views of sexuality in him as a boy—views that were but the projections of their own inner fears. Ultimately, anyone going through life with a load of resentment for some past action or inaction will discover that *by blessing those who seem to have caused their suffering*, they will soon be completely free, both of the suffering and of the resentment. It is a spiritual law. One day, they will discover with delight and joy that the old groove they were mentally programmed to accept has been totally effaced. No groove, no resentment (or regret, or remorse, or whatever the problem was).

UNLOADING YOUR PAST

I would like to suggest you try an exercise I have been doing for years in my "Recreating Your Life" workshops, with people from all walks of life. After a discussion on the past and the meaning of forgiveness and letting go, participants each receive a garbage bag in which they introduce a large stone (or stones) representing something in their past they wish to let go of or forgive: some long-held resentment, remorse, or regret. Often, if the stones are especially heavy, participants can double the bags, so they don't break!

Then they go off alone into nature, carrying their bag over their shoulder. The Alpine setting guarantees a steep slope for the walk. I ask them to ponder one simple fact: they are the person holding on to the bag, the bag isn't holding on to them! At any moment, the carrier can deposit the stone(s). With only two exceptions since I started these workshops, every single person put his or her stone down. Some participants have experienced ecstatic moments of liberation after depositing their stone, after realizing that the choice of letting go of the past or holding on to it was *theirs alone*.

One of the people who held on to the stone had a tremendous grudge against a former companion, who had abandoned her with two children. She said rather aggressively to my wife, "If he thinks I'm going to make him the free gift of depositing the stone . . ." Elly gently reminded the woman that she was carrying the stone, not her former companion! Three years later, she came back and participated in the same workshop—and finally deposited her stone.

We all move at our own speed. What counts is that we get there. On the spiritual level there is no fast or slow, because chronological time is an invention of the human mind, not a reality of the physical universe, as British physicist Julian Barbour, one of the scientific world's leading authorities on time, explains in his book *The End of Time*. Time is certainly no part of the spiritual universe, which is why some lessons that seem to come very slowly help us much more in our progression than others learned more rapidly.

Why not undertake the same exercise, alone, in nature? (Or at night if it's difficult for you to leave town.) It can be a very powerful experience. If possible, choose a rugged, uphill gradient. Just try. It will not cost you anything, and it could help you a lot.

Why carry the useless weight called "past" on the path of spiritual discovery, asks Eckhart Tolle in his book *The Power of Now*, which I consider the most profoundly original book on spiritual-ity to have appeared in the past fifty years. On a spiritual level, our only past is our present oneness with divine Love. And by our beliefs and attitudes, we create our future as surely as we entertain (or let go of) our past. That is why blessing each day and expecting good upon awakening are some of the most important rules for living, because the positive energy created by our blessings attracts good. (In the same manner, the negative energy created by fear attracts just the thing we feared!)

BLESSINGS OF HARDSHIP

I can already hear some readers protesting and saying, It's all very well for privileged Westerners to claim there exists a universal law of harmony. But what of whole populations living in conditions of extreme poverty? Are they not victims of circumstances they are quite incapable of influencing in any manner? Can you speak of the blessings of trials to people suffering from hunger, for instance?

These are difficult questions a book on spirituality cannot evade, especially if this book is claiming that universal spiritual laws exist—laws that are applicable everywhere, all the time, for everyone, whatever the circumstances.

However, at least some groups suffering from hunger have chosen to see trials as hidden blessings. And when they realize they need not see themselves as victims, astonishing things happen. In the 1980s, I undertook a trip of close to nine thousand miles through more than one hundred villages in tropical Africa and talked with thirteen hundred farmers—men and women—about what they were doing to help themselves. The result was the book *Listening to Africa: Developing Africa from the Grassroots*. Speaking of the immense challenges they had overcome in recent years, a peasant leader from Senegal commented, "Trials push us to innovate. It is because of these difficulties that the peasant initiatives were born. These difficulties have even been a good thing, for without them we would still be asleep."

In the village of Minti in the Dogon region of Mali, an area that suffered terribly from hunger in the eighties, the village chief, Dondo Peliaba, told me about a new technique the villagers had started using to combat soil erosion. Most of the families in Minti ate only one meal a day. At one moment, he remarked,

When abundance reigned, everyone was taking care of his own fields. Drought taught us to build small stone walls across our fields. We discovered plants that grow more rapidly. Before, we did not cultivate beans; now, they are one of our main staple crop. Hunger has become a teacher that has taught us to innovate, to think.

When Dondo Peliaba says that hunger has become a teacher, he is saying that life is a school, the universe a pedagogical laboratory, and that there is no meaningless suffering to those who wish to progress.

A still more striking example is that of the Committee to Fight for the End of Hunger (in French, COLUFIFA), created in the mid-eighties in southern Senegal. Serious problems of hunger hit this region, which was traditionally the bread (or rather rice) basket of Senegal. A peasant leader from the area, Demba Mansaré, gathered the farmers from the region to analyze the situation. After impassioned debates, and without condemning the government, the weather, fate, God, or the former colonial occupant, as they used to do automatically in the past, they asked the questions: What have we done (or not done) to allow such a situation to develop? *Where have we failed?*

They developed their own strategy of self-sufficiency, and for years worked harder than any peasant group I ever met during my many years working and living in Africa. They called aid the third hand—if it turns up, all the better. If not, we shall do without. Their slogan was a Senegalese proverb: The lack of means is already a means.

One of the original aspects of this group which struck me when I visited was that each meeting started with prayers and concluded with blessings. Imagine the scene: Here are some of the poorest among the world's poor, facing an acutely distressing situation, who take the time at each meeting to bless the Creator for the goodness toward them!

The advocates of a materialist vision of history claim that to uphold the idea of a fundamental law of harmony governing reality is the epitome of naïveté, sheer undiluted nonsense. They point to the dramatic condition of the world today, with its thirty-five thousand people dying of hunger per day, millions of children prostituting themselves to survive when they are not working as de facto slaves in carpet factories, the AIDS pandemic, and the close to three billion people—almost half the world's population—who survive on two dollars per day or less. And on and on. But the material vision of the world mediated by the senses may be a biased and incomplete vision of reality, for all we know. I would suggest advocates of this vision ponder the following luminous statement of Gary Zukav, who in his book *The Dancing Wu Li Masters*, writes,

> *The importance of nonsense hardly can be overstated. The more clearly we experience something as "nonsense," the more clearly we are experiencing the boundaries of our own self-imposed cognitive structures. "Nonsense" is that which does not fit into the prearranged patterns which we have superimposed*

on reality. There is no such thing as "nonsense," apart from a judgmental intellect which calls it that.

The second reply that can be given to the materialist vision of the universe—which is *as much an act of faith as that of the believer in a transcendent reality*—concerns our fundamental ignorance of the manner in which the universe functions and our basic ignorance concerning the nature of ultimate, or "real," reality. Ask any serious scientist what percentage his knowledge represents of the totality of knowledge in the universe (which might be called omniscience). He will look at you with humor or irony and will quote a figure which could be in the order of 0.000 . . . 0001 percent. Even the sum total of accumulated scientific knowledge (which only represents a fraction of accumulated *human* knowledge) will still be, relatively speaking, close to this figure.

Faced with the abysmal extent of our ignorance, is it not a much more absurd and irrational attitude to make the *a priori* claim that such a fundamental law of harmony does not exist? Would it not be more intelligent and—yes—more scientific to accept the working hypothesis of the existence of such a law and take it as the basis of our action (expressed, for instance, in the art of blessing)? We would then attempt to see what happens when we systematically experiment with blessing. This is the approach I would suggest to readers willing and capable of setting their materialistic biases aside.

The Swedish sociologist Gunnar Myrdal once commented,

Facts do not organize themselves into concepts and theories just by being looked at; indeed, except within the framework of concepts and theories, there are no scientific facts but only chaos.

— independent of experience

There is an inescapable a priori element in all scientific work. Questions must be asked before answers can be given. The questions are expressions of our interest in the world, they are at bottom valuations.

What if we had asked the wrong question?

What if the senses—sight, hearing, touch, etc., upon which are based almost all modern scientific research—far from revealing the key to reality, were hiding it, as some of the great teachings of the spiritual wisdom of humankind have proclaimed since the beginning of time? The fact that numerous scientists refuse to envisage such a possibility, *even as a temporary working hypothesis,* is a rather unscientific attitude! Indeed, it is because I have a scientific training and such a profound faith in the scientific method that I feel the need to raise the issue. "Woe unto he, who at least once in his life, has not put everything into question" wrote the French thinker Blaise Pascal, centuries ago.

"There is a dream dreaming us," a Bushman once said to Laurens van der Post, the British writer of South African origin. And if that dream were matter? And if material existence itself were just one great dream? To refuse to consider this eventuality because it would upset too many apple carts, not to mention most of modern science, is hardly a satisfying answer for a truly independent thinker.

So, this is the question we will ponder in the following chapter.

On Your Path to Blessing

*What lessons might be presenting themselves
repeatedly in your life? What will it take to
learn them?*

*Are there any hardships you've experienced
that you now see as blessings?
The next time you're in a difficult situation,
try blessing with the knowledge that we
all, no exceptions, are governed by a law
of universal harmony.*

9

THE DEEPER MEANING OF THE ART OF BLESSING

To bless means to wish, unconditionally and from the deepest chamber
of your heart, unrestricted good for others and events; it means to
hallow, to hold in reverence, to behold with awe that which is always a
gift from the Creator. He who is hallowed by your blessing is set aside,
consecrated, holy, whole. To bless is to invoke divine care upon,
to speak or think gratefully for, to confer happiness upon, although
we ourselves are never the bestower but simply the joyful
witnesses of life's abundance.

In the last few chapters we have discussed the spiritual laws that are called into effect by conscious blessing. Now let us turn our attention to integrating this gentle art into your daily life and your own spiritual practice, whatever that may be.

Blessing is much more an attitude of deep reverence than words, more an authentic and profound aspiration of the heart than a mechanically repeated formula which is part of a religious ritual. Yet the latter is what the word *blessing* has come to mean for most people. Too often, such rituals of blessing have lost all meaning and have become pure form with no substance. As a friend told me when I was writing this book, "In my youth, blessing was something reserved for priests. I would never for a second have thought of blessing someone." Fortunately, there is no monopoly of caste or creed on blessing!

The study of the spiritual practices of humanity shows that the art of blessing is practiced by all sorts of people from all walks of life. No formal consecration is needed, no church authorization, no theological degree of any sort. Just a sincere heart. It can become something as natural as breathing and talking.

In its deepest meaning, blessing means understanding and rejoicing that the being we are blessing is in a state of grace, of total freedom and innocence in front of its Creator, and that this being's cup overflows, as Psalm 23 states.

Experiencing the Deeper Meaning of Blessing

Blessing as defined in this book can be a powerful tool in all sorts of emergency situations. The day before starting work on the manuscript of this book, I was walking with my godchild, Jacqueline, along Lake Geneva. Since the morning, I had been feeling very uneasy on a spiritual level. I felt invaded by all manner of evil mental attacks. During our walk, we met a young woman who was holding on to a bush, muttering to herself, in a state of evident distress. In addition to being drunk, she seemed to suffer from some kind of drug overdose. We asked if we could help her, but after a brief exchange of words, she left abruptly, walking with difficulty.

Jacqueline and I sat on a bench and started blessing this unknown young woman. Suddenly, I felt a deep assurance, as clear as it was unshakable, that on another level of being and consciousness existing simultaneously with ours, this young woman was totally loved, surrounded, cherished, cared for, protected, and blessed. Immediately afterward, the state of mental confusion I had felt since the morning vanished completely.

Each of us can have such experiences, no matter where we are. Eileen Caddy explains that at one time in her life, she lived in a small caravan with her husband, Peter, their friend Dorothy, and three children. In this cramped setting, she found it difficult to meditate and listen to God. Nonetheless, she prayed and relayed to me,

> *I was told in my guidance to go to the public toilet to meditate. There were three sections and I would go in the third so as not to disturb people. I used to get the most wonderful guidance in the public toilet. It taught me that God is within. I find a lot of mothers who say: But I have children, and I can't possibly find time to pray. I say: I'm sorry. I don't accept that. If you want something badly enough, you will make time for it, even if it means getting up an hour earlier. You will do that. It all depends on your priorities, what you are putting first. As Jesus said, "Seek ye first the kingdom of God, and all the rest shall be added unto you." I accept that completely. When you give God all, He gives all—and much more—in return.*

I especially love this experience, which Eileen shared with me in a long interview, because it completely destroys the holier-than-thou vision of a pseudospirituality in which form and environment are more important than substance, a spirituality attached to a "house of prayer," all sorts of mental and physical postures, expiatory rituals, readings, and so on, practiced at specific moments in a rigidly defined manner. Either spirituality is integrated into the most humdrum or normal daily activities, from washing up to love relationships, from jogging to shopping, or it is not even worth mentioning. Above all, true spirituality is a way of being.

Such blessing is exemplified by Ram Dass's story of a young American who ventures to Japan to study martial arts. He is riding the subway, and at one station an immense, completely drunk, unsavory-looking hulk of a man enters the subway car. He aggressively jostles various passengers and violently pushes a woman down the aisle. At this point, the young American feels compelled to act. For the first time, he finds himself in a situation where he can apply in real life the skills he has mastered in the martial arts classroom through years of training. When the drunken hulk hurls insults at him, he steps forward, poised to defend the widow and the orphan and to teach the drunkard a lesson he will not forget.

At that pivotal moment, a tiny, elderly gentleman sitting on a seat with his tiny wife, lets out a piercing shout. The drunkard, completely taken aback, turns around. Then the old gentleman beckons him, inviting him to sit down beside him. He starts talking to the huge fellow—who must have been twice his size—of his love for *sake* (rice wine). He has found a common link with the drunken man. After a few moments, they are talking to each other like old friends. The giant starts to cry. All aggressiveness has melted. He becomes like a child.

At this point, the young American realizes that the old man has just given him an extraordinary lesson in martial arts: that the ultimate of this art is to never use it—physically; that the only real victory is the victory over self, be it fear, anger, or self-justification. He exits the subway car, taking with him the image of a huge man with his head on the knees of a neat, kindly old gentleman who is caressing his dirty, matted hair.

The old man was blessing his neighbor without pronouncing anything but the most ordinary words. He had gone far beyond talking *about* spiritual truths. He was simply being love.

That is the supreme blessing.

On Your Path to Blessing

What has blessing meant to you in the past?
What does it mean to you now?
Do you ever feel as though you don't have time
to devote to your spirituality?
What could you do to make your spirituality a
way of being?

10
A NEW WAY OF
SEEING AND BELIEVING

To bless is to acknowledge the omnipresent,
universal beauty hidden from material eyes; it is to activate
that law of attraction which, from the furthest reaches of the universe,
will bring into your life exactly what you need to experience and enjoy.

Most scientists would probably agree that love exists. But who has ever physically seen the substance of this thing called love which has motivated such a great proportion of human action for aeons?

Who has ever weighed, measured, dissected love? Who has loaded it into a computer, verified its reliability in a laboratory, given it a warrant of authenticity or an official certificate of origin? Has anyone ever described its chemical or molecular structure? Analyzed its reaction time to various stimuli while maintaining consistency among key variables? Made statistically significant predictions concerning its response to specific conditions of stress, or plotted its development on a Gauss curve? (Normal Bell Shaped Curve)

Has anyone ever been able to purchase true love? Can it be stored in a safe or introduced into a portfolio of top-rated investment funds? And what interest rate would you put on love?

Obviously, these are impossible questions. Yet is love less real because we cannot classify, calculate, catalog, stock, measure, file, weigh, summarize, register, patent, or sell it?

No one, apart from a few confused or dogmatic wanderers in the desert of extreme materialism, would claim love does not exist or attempt to reduce it to mere chemical stimuli. But if we accept that true love exists—not the unstable desire or the fragile narcissism which sometimes passes for love, but the true thing, strong, unchanging, unconditional, universal in its unlimited generosity—what is its substance? Its source? Where does it abide? In the left ventricle of the heart (or the right one if you are conservative)? In a given area of your brain? In the electric current that teases your skin in a caress or at the tip of your tongue waiting to be awakened by a kiss?

Certainly it is in a mother's all-night vigil over a feverish child. It is reflected in a father's face when he sees his daughter going out of the door, light as a moon ray, to her first school dance. But there is more to love than this.

Love is an infinite force for good, a *healing* force.

To understand it in its fullness requires unconventional perception, new ways of seeing and being. And just as love cannot be quantified, so it is with blessing. Their intangible nature makes them no less real.

INFLUENCES THAT SHAPE OUR REALITY

Deepak Chopra tells the story of an experiment conducted at Harvard University many years ago. Two groups of kittens were raised from birth to early adulthood in two rooms. The walls of one room were painted in black and white vertical stripes, those in the other room with horizontal stripes. Once set free, the young cats brought up in the room with horizontal stripes knocked into everything vertical—chair and table legs, trees, poles—because they were incapable of discerning anything upright. Their neuronal structures had organized themselves around a world of horizontal stripes.

In a way, we are like these young cats. We have been brought up to filter all "reality" through the senses. Or rather, we normally call reality that which we can feel, touch, taste, smell, and see. Furthermore, even in the physical world, we tend to see only what our culture, social environment, education (be it scientific or theological), and prejudices have trained us to see. A Wall Street banker parachuted into the Kalahari desert would not last long. A Kalahari Bushman dropped into the Bronx—probably not much longer. Each would be blinded by his own cultural upbringing to the resources available in environments previously unknown to him.

In 1520, when Ferdinand Magellan arrived at the Tierra del Fuego, at the tip of South America, what surprised him and his crew was that the Del Fuego Indians, who lived around the bay, had not spotted his boats entering the bay. He realized that nothing in their past cultural experience had prepared them for the idea of vessels that (to them) resembled huge floating houses. They were used to tiny canoes, not ships. Canoes represented the reality and completely sealed their imagination, hence their vision. He liberated their vision by taking them onto his ships.[1]

Another of countless examples of how our environment and experience shapes our view appears in Martin and Inge Goldstein's 1978 book, *How We Know*—on the scientific method. The authors tell what happened when, for the first time, thanks to a new surgical technique, people born blind because of cataracts were able to see. Just after the successful operation, patients saw nothing but "spinning masses of lights and colors." They were quite incapable of picking out or naming specific objects. They were not even aware of a space containing various specific objects. They all had to undergo a long training because their brains had not been trained in the rules of seeing. As the authors concluded,

> It is apparent that [sight]—the sense we think of as most directly putting us in touch with facts—is learned rather than automatic. We see with our minds, not with our eyes, and we are subject to whatever unconscious biases and misconceptions are produced by the training that teaches us to see ... things need not be what they seem ... changes in our own thinking may change what we see.

wow!

Our interpretation, our filtering of reality through the senses, cannot give us the key to reality, because from the millions of sensory micro-data that bombard us every second, we do not have the ability to build a holistic vision of things (in the true sense of the term: embracing the totality of reality). Deepak Chopra has gone so far as to say that the sensation and substance of the world surrounding us is a form of socially programmed hypnotism or mesmerism, a convenient fiction of which we are all prisoners. Coming from someone with a rigorous scientific training, such statements are quite startling!

COSMIC CONSCIOUSNESS

Research undertaken since the beginning of the past century in the field of quantum physics, and since the mid-century in other areas, points to the fact that we live in a universe based on energy. In numerous fields, from physics to neurology, from psychosomatic medicine to environmental sciences, authorized voices in growing numbers are questioning the materialistic premises of our old paradigm. In the spectrum of literature relating to the nature of reality, all these voices and many others suggest that energy, thought, *consciousness* may well constitute the ultimate texture or substance of the universe. What the English philosopher-mathematician Bertrand Russell once called "omnipotent matter" comes across more and more as a rather flimsy, vacillating, and transitory phenomenon!

Let us define *true substance*[2] as something permanent, intangible, fundamentally harmonious, and incapable of decaying. If matter is not true substance, might not the latter then consist of ideas? Rather than kings and bankers, tanks and technologies, might not the real actors of history be ideas and thoughts, and even blessings? What if this other, nonmaterial reality were as close to us as our thoughts?

In 1969, Oxford University created the Religious Experience Research Centre. There's nothing very extraordinary in that—except that its founder was an internationally renowned professor of zoology, Sir Alister Hardy, who decided to extend his research beyond crocodiles and koalas.[3] The first book published by this center, *The Spiritual Nature of Man*, describes a vast field of experiences related to a reality beyond that of everyday normality, i.e., what we experience through the five senses and what we are educated to accept as "true". These experiences point to the existence of very different states of consciousness that fundamentally transform our perception of reality. Mystics have been speaking about such things for centuries, even millennia, but to see these states confirmed by scientists with a more hard-nosed approach opens up new perspectives. What is particularly interesting is to see how many people—sometimes very ordinary people, your news anchor, bus driver, or pharmacist—have had such experiences.

A typical experience quoted in the book is that of a young student traveling by train in England. He was in a "dingy, third-class compartment," in the company of very modest people, when suddenly,

for a few seconds only, I suppose, the whole compartment was filled with light. This is the only way I know in which to describe the moment, for there was nothing to see at all. I felt caught up into some tremendous sense of being within a loving, triumphant, and shining purpose. I never felt more humble. I never felt more exalted. . . . I felt that all was well for mankind—how poor the words seem! The word "well" is so poverty stricken. All men were shining and glorious beings who in the end would enter incredible joy. Beauty, music, joy, love immeasurable, and a glory unspeakable, all this they would inherit. Of this they were heirs.

The world's mystical literature is replete with passages in the same vein, describing another reality, a parallel universe of a perfection and harmony which defies all normal, verbal expression. Numerous examples of suddenly changed perception can be found in the classic *Cosmic Consciousness*, first published in the late 1890s by a Canadian alienist (alienists were the predecessors to psychiatrists) of international repute, Richard Maurice Bucke, MD. For a time that might have been a few minutes to a few weeks, the people whose experiences this author describes were able to escape from the culturally conditioned programming of perception we all submit to, day after day, year after year. Bucke undertook a detailed study of this cosmic consciousness, both in world literature and his own practice, as he had himself been through one such experience, and it changed his life.

I would like to quote at length one of the testimonies from his book. It is especially interesting, because it explains well the fundamental oneness of all things in the universe and insists that the basic structure of the universe is completely harmonious. (This is a common characteristic of such experiences in many religions and cultures.) The text is all the more compelling because it was written by a simple mother and housewife who saw herself as an agnostic.

Speaking of the manner in which her cosmic experience started, she writes,

It seemed so simple and natural (with all the wonder of it) that I and my affairs went on as usual. The light and color glowed, the atmosphere seemed to quiver and vibrate around and within me. Perfect rest and peace and joy were everywhere, and, more strange than all, there came to me a sense as of some serene, magnetic presence—grand and all pervading. . . . I was seeing and comprehending the sublime meaning of things, the reasons for all that had been hidden and dark. The great truth that life is a spiritual evolution, that this life is but a passing phase in the soul's progression, burst upon my astonished vision with overwhelming grandeur. Oh, I thought, if this is what it means, if this is the outcome, then pain is sublime! Welcome centuries, eons, of suffering if it brings us to this! And still the splendor increased. Presently, what seemed to be a swift, oncoming tidal

incapable of being expressed in words

wave of splendor and glory <u>ineffable</u> came down upon me, and I felt myself being enveloped, swallowed up. . . .

Now came a period of rapture so intense that the universe stood still, as if amazed at the unutterable majesty of the spectacle! Only one in all the infinite universe! The All-loving, the Perfect One! The Perfect Wisdom, truth, love and purity! And with the rapture came the insight. In that same wonderful moment of what might be called <u>supernal</u> bliss, came illumination. I saw with intense inward vision the atoms or molecules, of which seemingly the universe is composed—I know not whether material or spiritual—rearranging themselves, as the cosmos (in its continuous everlasting life) passes from order to order. What joy when I saw there was no break in the chain—not a link left out—everything in its place and time. Worlds, systems, all blended in one harmonious whole. Universal life synonymous with universal love!

being or coming from on high

How long that period of intense rapture lasted I do not know—it seemed an eternity—it might have been but a few moments. Then came relaxation, the happy tears, the murmured, rapturous expression. I was safe; I was on the great highway, the upward road which humanity had trod with bleeding feet, but with deathless hope in the heart, and songs of love and trust on the lips. . . . In the morning, I awoke with a slight headache, but with the spiritual sense so strong that what we call the actual, material things surrounding me seemed shadowy and unreal. My point of view was entirely changed. Old things had passed away and all had become new. . . . Every longing of the heart was satisfied, *every* question answered, the "pent-up, aching rivers" had reached the ocean—I loved infinitely and was infinitely loved! The universal tide flowed in

*upon me in waves of joy and gladness, pouring down over me
as in torrents of fragrant balm. . . .*

*That sweet eternal smile on nature's face! There is nothing
in the universe to compare with it—such joyous repose and
sweet unconcern—saying to us, with tenderest love: All is well,
always has been and will always be. . . . It was the gladness and
rapture of love, so intensified that it became an ocean of living,
palpitating light, the brightness of which outshone the brightness
of the sun. Its glow, warmth and tenderness filling the universe.
That infinite ocean was eternal love, the soul of nature and all
one endless smile! . . .*

We think we see, but we are really blind—if we could see! . . .

*Out of this experience was born an unfaltering trust. Deep
in the soul, below pain, below all the distraction of life, is a
silence vast and grand—an infinite ocean of calm, which nothing can disturb; Nature's own exceeding peace which "passes
understanding."*

*That which we seek with passionate longing, here and
there, upward and outward, we find at last within ourselves.
The kingdom within! The indwelling God!*

The idea of an infinite spiritual harmony behind the grimac-
ing, discordant mask of material appearances is a recurring theme
in what we call, for want of a better term, mystical literature, and
which we might simply call trans-material perception—perception
that pierces the veil of the hypnotic screen of matter. Bucke's tes-
tifier echoes almost word for word the accounts of the great English mystic Julian of Norwich, who was accustomed to repeating
over and over again "all shall be well, and all shall be well, and all
manner of things shall be well."

THE WORLD BEYOND OUR EYES

And what if the material world really were a mesmeric seeming—
a dream dreaming us?

According to the Copenhagen school of physics, founded by
the Danish physicist Neils Bohr, who is one of the fathers of quantum physics, there is no "real" world independent of the observer.
As physicist David Merman once explained not without humor,
we know that the moon is not there when no one's looking at it!
Not all physicists would agree with this interpretation. (Nowadays,
there is almost as much disagreement among scientists as among
theologians!) However, it is sufficiently widespread to warrant serious consideration.

If all that we see is filtered and interpreted through our consciousness, can the world even exist outside of our perception of
things? Maybe the most important intuition we can have concerning the world or reality is that *all is consciousness*. We create our
reality by the way we perceive things.

Visionaries, poets, and seers of all times and hues claim that
there exists an omnipresent beauty hidden to material eyes. As we
learn to bless despite all appearances, we will slowly become more
and more aware of this other reality, for we see with our thoughts
before seeing with our eyes.

Blessing is a way of opening up to life, especially this reality
beyond what we see. As we bless our day upon awakening, we
open ourselves to receiving all we need. This fundamental harmony behind the veil of material appearances comes into our life
via a universal law of good, which delivers unto us precisely what
we need to progress at this very moment of our existence, in
exactly the manner we need in order to go forward.

An example of this is furnished by a Swede, Tord, who shared at an international meeting held in Boston how he had experienced healing of very serious ills simply by blessing others all day long. Tord is a member of the Christian Science movement, a teaching that has been healing all manner of disease with remarkable effectiveness for over 125 years. His testimony was sent to me by a friend who received it from him. In it, Tord recounts how this teaching transformed his life:

From a big hell to a very big heaven . . . I was a very fat person with very bad eyesight and had to be interned at a mental hospital many times because of psychiatric disorders. Fifteen years ago, when I was to get my driver's license, it was found I had very bad eyesight, so I contacted a Christian Science practitioner [someone who heals by prayer alone] in my hometown. I asked her what I should do. She told me not to accept glasses because eyesight is spiritual, and that divine Love always keeps my sight in full harmony, and that I really saw with God's eyes. She told me to be kind to all, and that she would pray for me.

So I started to bless people. Whenever I met someone, I would think, "God bless you." I did this from morning till evening. When I had done this for about three months, for a short while I suddenly could read the names of ships on the ocean, which I couldn't do before. This gave me an enormous inspiration. I went on blessing people still more than before, and started to help ladies across the street, whether they wanted it or not. Fourteen days later, I was sitting at home reading the [Christian Science] textbook when suddenly a very strong light filled my mind. This was the Christ coming to me. It lasted for

*ten minutes, then disappeared. Two months later, this light
began to flow more and more frequently, and I am sure that
nothing can stop it.*

*I became a very harmonious person, and my obesity disap-
peared. My eyesight has been restored, and the mental illness
has disappeared. Sometimes, I feel I am the happiest person in
the world. I am sure this spiritual light will by and by fill every
one in the world with love and holiness so that we can come out
from matter and darkness and reach our spiritual minds.* . . .
I can't express my gratitude enough. . . . *Jesus said "Heaven is
near." Actually, it really is within us.*

This is one more example of the power of constant blessing
and how its consecrated practice brought complete healing to
someone with severe mental and physical problems.

More and more, contemporary research is showing how our
view of things is essentially subjective. Byron Katie, in her seminal
book *A Thousand Names for Joy*, tells us that ultimate reality is perfect and that learning to love what is constitutes the best path to
become aware of this perfection:

*When the mind believes what it thinks, it names what cannot be
named and tries to make it real through a name. It believes that
its names are real, that there's a world out there separate from
itself. That's an illusion. The whole world is projected. When
you're shut down and frightened, the world seems hostile; when
you love what is, everything in the world becomes the beloved.
Inside and outside always match.* . . . *The world is the mirror
image of your own mind.*

The act of blessing situations, people, and events is one of the most meaningful ways of enhancing this awareness, of seeing everything in the light, as the beloved.

On Your Path to Blessing

*What cultural or environmental filters have
shaped your version of reality?
Have you stopped to think what may lie behind
what you perceive with your senses?
Craft a blessing intended to open yourself up
to this hidden reality.*

NOTES

1. Cousins, Norman, "The U.S. Constitution," *The Christian Science Monitor*, September 17, 1987. Concerning the Del Fuego Indians.

2. In his seminal study *Teaching as a Conserving Activity* (New York: Delta Book, 1979) 159, Neil Postman writes that "definitions, like questions and metaphors, are instruments for thinking. Their authority rests entirely on their usefulness, not their correctness."

3. For a general presentation of mysticism, the seminal study of Evelyn Underhill, *Mysticism: A Study in the Nature and Development of Man's Spiritual Consciousness* is excellent. This comprehensive study was first published in 1911 and remains a classic in the field of religious literature.

11

SEEING THE HIDDEN GOOD

When you pass a hospital, bless its patients in their present wholeness,
for even in their suffering, their wholeness awaits discovery within them.
When your eyes behold a man in tears or seemingly broken by life,
bless him in his vitality and joy, for the material senses present
but the inverted image of the ultimate splendor and perfection
that only the inner eye beholds.
When you pass a prison, mentally bless its inmates in their innocence
and freedom, their gentleness, pure essence, and unconditional
forgiveness; for one can only be a prisoner of one's self-image, and a
free man can walk unshackled in jail, just as citizens of a free country
may be prisoners of the fear lurking within their thoughts.

To see the good where the contrary seems to exist is certainly not playing Pollyanna. Nor is affirming innocence and health where corruption and disease seem to reign. It is based on the spiritual fact that even a modest grasp of the spiritual perfection underlying the universe can be manifested in transformed lives and physical healings. That is the idea behind seeing the hidden good, and you can do this easily through blessing, no matter how challenging the object of your blessing may be.

An ancient Hindu story tells of a time when all men were gods. But they so abused their divinity that Brahman, the master of the gods, decided to take away their divine power and hide it in a place where they would never think of looking for it. So the great problem was: where could he hide it?

The minor gods were convened to seek a solution to this problem. They said, "Let's hide man's divinity in the soil." But Brahman replied: no use. "Man will dig the fields and find it."

The gods then replied, "In that case, let's throw man's divinity to the bottom of the deepest ocean." Again Brahman replied that sooner or later, man would explore the oceans and finally find it.

Whereupon the minor gods concluded, "We can't think of any place on earth where man might not one day think of looking for it!"

Brahman then said: "Here is what we will do with the divinity of man: We will hide it deep in himself, for that is the only place where he will never think of looking for it."

Since then, concludes the legend, man has circled the earth. He has explored, climbed, plunged, and dug in his search for something that is in his heart. When we bless, we are affirming the good that is within all of us.

When Beauty Is Hard to See

Deep inside the most hardened criminal, the most cruel tyrant, the most indifferent, cynical, disillusioned person resides infinite and hidden beauty—which that person is often the first to ignore. The following story taken from *A Century of Christian Science Healing* illustrates this affirmation with a concrete example. The narrator is an English officer who directed a naval detention center for rebellious conscripts and deserters during World War II. One day, the center received a particularly difficult case, a violent man court-martialed as a habitual deserter. This inmate ran foul of all forms of authority, smashing everything in his cell (window and light included), even tearing his uniform to shreds. He would

strike the staff at the first opportunity and simply refused to cooperate. His behavior was completely antisocial—an extreme case of
rebellion against all forms of discipline. Punishments seemed to
have no effect on him whatsoever.

The officer explained that the psychiatrist, chaplain, school-
teacher, and he had all attempted in vain to reason with the man.
All human means having failed, the director then decided to
attempt a spiritual approach, and he prayed three hours nonstop
for the inmate. He was led to go back to the prison, feeling that he
was going with the power of the Spirit, yet not knowing what to
do. Just before midnight, he called the guard to unlock the cell,
and then sent him on his rounds. His story continues:

*Upon going in, I saw the man still on the floor, motionless.
I went over to him in the dim light and stood over him. The
thought came to me, Right there is the son of God. I held
this thought to the best of my ability for fifteen minutes; neither
of us said a word. I then went out and called the warden to go
in and release him, give him a wash, some fresh clothes, and
his bed, and turn him in.*

The next day, the man was completely transformed. He was
"friendly and obedient to regulations." He had to stand trial for an
injury inflicted on someone before coming to the prison, and he
was condemned to two years in a civil prison. Later, the director
received a letter from the inmate thanking the personnel of the
prison for what they had done for him. A man who had arrived
spewing hatred and venom had been transformed into a new person because someone had cared enough to affirm and spiritually
maintain with total conviction his hidden inner perfection.

AFFIRMING DIVINITY IN EXTREME SITUATIONS

Perhaps the most remarkable example I know of reversing appearances occurred during the tragic 1994 civil war in Rwanda, which claimed the lives of eight hundred thousand people. The account was told to one of my closest friends by the person involved, an African spiritual healer who managed to neutralize a band of ethnic murderers through the might of Spirit—through the understanding of the essential spiritual nature of our true being and an unshakable conviction of the superiority of spiritual law over all material obstacles. The would-be murderers had broken into his house in the middle of the night intending to massacre his whole family:

> One night, around two in the morning, in the middle of the civil war, an armed band entered my home. I awoke to see what was happening, and we met nose to nose in the corridor. They were armed with guns and bayonets, I was armed with Truth and Love. As they pointed their weapons to menace me, a thought came to me in a flash, immediately dispelling the fear which was attempting to invade my thought. Love and Life are indestructible and permanent. I am the idea of Life, God, indestructible in Life, permanent in my being! There is only one Life, God, which remains undivided, not two or more lives. This infinite Life is the life of these so-called killers, my life, and that of my family.

For long moments, this man continued to make spiritual affirmations based on his unwavering conviction that spiritual laws exist that enable us to meet all situations, whatever they are, and heal us through the power of truth.

Quite a few times, disaster seemed imminent. When at one moment one of his daughters started crying, the head of the band gave the order to kill her. Without even pronouncing a word out loud, the healer immediately affirmed that the man who had received the order to kill was the perfect child of divine Love. "The law of Love which is present here, controls this situation and governs each and everyone."[1] Immediately, the man who had already raised his bayonet to pierce the girl interrupted his gesture.

Each moment of this trial was precious for me. I did not allow myself the slightest mental distraction to see the problem from a material angle. I constantly maintained my thought on the level of true spiritual reality. . . . After working spiritually for about thirty minutes, these men became very calm, as if feeling the love we reflected. Their chief called them, and they left our room. This gave me time to affirm still more forcefully absolute truths about the perfect man of God's creation.[2]

Once back in the room, these men were transformed. They had become new persons. Even their language had completely changed. They were disarmed and friendly, and started confessing the crimes they had committed. They stayed at our home for two hours. No one was hurt; everybody was safe and sound.

This story is truly stunning.[3] Yet did not Jesus state that in his name (in other words, in the power of the Spirit and the unconditional Love he lived) we would do miracles greater than his? Are we ready to accept the challenge?

Blessing to reverse appearances doesn't have to be applied only to situations as incredible as the ones I've mentioned. Miracles can be found in the mundane as well, such as seeing the divinity in the person who cuts you off in traffic, or blessing people in their resourcefulness and abundance when you hear dismal economic news on the television. You may be surprised by the results.

On Your Path to Blessing

Have you ever passed up chances to affirm
good in the face of the contrary?
If so, what could you have thought instead to
reverse the appearance?
In what ways can you affirm good through
your blessings in your daily life?

NOTES

1. The narrator is speaking of the divine universe, not the world of material appearances which had invaded his house. We come back here to the idea that all is consciousness. On the level of the material circumstances revealed by sight and sound, it was apparently hell for his family and him. On another, parallel level, that of his higher spiritual awareness, love reigned supreme.

2. The writer refers here to the first chapter of Genesis, which states twice that "God created man in his own image"—hence, perfect.

3. The written story was given to me by a close African friend, Emery Tazuila, to whom it was told by the person concerned, Makengo Ma Pululu, who was living in Rwanda at the time.

12

DON'T FORGET TO BLESS YOURSELF

P.S. And of course, above all,
do not forget to bless the utterly beautiful person you are.

Dear friend, have you ever thought about what a unique and wonderful person you are? Thought about it in the etymological sense of the word *wonderful*: a person full of beautiful things to behold, to marvel about? Have you ever thought how deeply cherished of the universe, of Providence you are? Have you ever considered that the reality known to us by convention or education as God spends Her time blessing you and just rejoicing that you exist? In the words of a famous visionary Zephaniah (3:17), "The Lord thy God in the midst of thee is mighty; he will save, he will rejoice over thee with joy; he will rest in his love, he will joy over thee with singing." Have you ever thought of your Creator just being so happy about your existence that She's practically dancing for joy?

Have you, moreover, asked yourself that if you find it so difficult to imagine an infinitely good Deity rejoicing over you—rather than the Deity who is misinformed about who you *really* are deep down—you might be the one who is mistaken about your own identity?

Have you ever realized the meaning of the following?

🌱 The principle of infinite harmony and love governing the universe is intensely concerned about your happiness and just will not let you go until you have reached total bliss and infinite fulfillment.

🌱 The responsibility of this supreme being is binding and it will honor its commitment to your supreme happiness and total bliss till the very end.

So while we've spent most of this book discussing how and why to bless others, it is equally important to bless yourself. Remember that, whatever the representation you may have of yourself, deep inside you exists a space of infinite beauty and rest, of total unconditional Love, of goodness without bounds, of unshakable peace and calm, of dancing joy and playful being, of limitless vision and infinite abundance.

This space constitutes our true being. No event in life—no crippling disease, torment, suffering, or childhood traumas, absolutely nothing—will ever mar its wholeness, which constitutes our true identity. Little wonder God rejoices over us, over you, with singing, if that's what She sees. Maybe it's time to start seeing ourselves as She sees us. Blessing yourself will help you greatly along the way.

Does this sound too good to be true? Even your disbelief cannot change the spiritual fact of creatures made in divine Love's image. As you hold on to this truth with a deep yearning to understand and *feel* it (because truth has to be felt, not just known), you will become aware of it little by little and see it manifested in your life. Moment by moment we have that glorious, incredible choice: to see ourselves as miserable sinners or to accept ourselves as children of the light. "Do not doubt your own inner splendor. Each living being is a star," states Tibetan master Dugpa Rinpoche.

So, day in and day out, hour after hour, bless the absolutely wonderful person you are in your true nature, which is likely very different from the outward masks you wear—masks that often deceive even the wearer! We cannot really love our neighbor until we have learned to love ourselves, and blessing ourselves is one of the privileged paths of this apprenticeship.

One of my favorite descriptions of our inner splendor is in American poet Doris Peel's words, which can be read as a beautiful commentary on the passage from Zephaniah quoted above:

Daily I am His delight
Daily He rejoices in
His handiwork—
all fresh, all bright,
all wrought from elemental light
to be what He beholds as me.
His song sung out in world this day!
His theme in play! His act of joy!
Love laughs. And
O it is laughter
that I am! His poem, His psalm!

In sight of Him
how fashioned of gladness
I must be! How lark-on-wing
A thing that—That He
daily should thus
delight in me: His poem, His song
sung out, His theme!

His everlasting act
of joy.

I can imagine a reader saying, "Come on, man. You can't mean it. I'm in my balding fifties and an alcoholic, divorced three times, heavily in debt. My self-esteem is at rock-bottom—and you want me to love and bless myself?" And another: "My husband has just dumped me for his secretary and left me with three adolescent kids, one on drugs. The princess who used to be the beauty queen of her school is a heavy, very bitter middle-aged divorcée, struggling to barely survive . . . and you want me to feel love for this creature?" Or again, "My life is, outwardly, a brilliant success. But inwardly, I'm a shambles, and my existence is just one great big lie, and you want me to bless the apocalyptic mess called me?"

I don't feel I have the right to tell a single individual on the planet what she or he should think or do. Yet this poem encourages us all to delve deeper, below the surface appearance of things, and accept the idea of the space of inner beauty described above as reflecting the *real* us, a self completely untouched by the circumstances of life. Might you accept it as a working hypothesis? And then see what happens!

For many years, each time I committed some mistake, manifested clumsiness, blundered in any way (such as breaking a dish, or forgetting something important), I used to curse myself, telling myself what a fool or what a prime idiot I was. (We each have our private repertoire of unkindnesses aimed at ourselves!) Then one day I realized that this constant harping at myself only reinforced the old subconscious programs of self-condemnation. I was, very literally, programming myself for unhappiness and lack of self-esteem. So one day, I simply reversed the process and started blessing myself. Now, if I'm clumsy, or forgetful, or whatever, I bless myself in my dexterity, alertness, or perfect memory; if I get angry, I bless myself in my poise. And because I condemn myself less, I condemn others less also. It is all so simple. Not always easy, by any means—but simple.

A very dear friend who read the manuscript of this book shared the following real-life experience with me:

For years I have been doing what you describe [blessing]—but not toward myself, and for me this was the real eye-opener in your pages. It is thrilling to bless oneself in the way you describe. Somehow it feels so different from simply declaring oneself as "God's perfect child.".... It feels more specific, embracing, liberating. I think it is due to the focus you put on unconditional Love and on the idea that we are all God's presence.

Two days ago I had a marvelous little experience with this when I left home to do a few errands. Opening the car door, I saw several things on the driver's seat that needed to be moved before I could sit down. So I put my large purse/briefcase on the hood of the car and then reached inside to move things from the driver's seat to the back seat. Then I got into the car and drove off, forgetting about my bag.

She then drove twelve miles before becoming aware, at her first stop, of the absence of her bag. She started really berating herself for being so careless. The fact that the bag contained not only her credit cards, license, $150 in cash, but also some important papers made her all the more angry with herself:

> I decided to drive back home, following the same route, keeping my eyes open for the bag. After going about one hundred meters, fuming all the way, I suddenly thought of the gentle art of blessing. What a huge shift in thought! Immediately I began blessing myself in my alertness, attentiveness, care, love of order. I remembered that as evidence of God's presence, of Principle's presence, I possess all of those qualities; they are inherent in my being. I felt alight with these thoughts, liberated, joyous. Yet by the time I turned onto my street, I had seen no trace of the bag. Nor did I see it in the driveway. Thinking that I might have left it in the house, I got out of the car to go inside. And what did I find propped up against the front door? My now very dirty bag. Clearly, it had fallen off the car along the road and someone had stopped to pick it up, found the ID/address card, and hand-delivered it to my door with all contents intact. Of course I was delighted to find the bag, but I was thrilled to find myself, my true self, through blessing. Moreover, the person who had returned my bag had done so in secret—leaving no name or number. So, to express my gratitude, I will just have to bless every person I pass for their integrity, knowing that any one of them might be my benefactor.

LOVING YOURSELF

Arnaud Desjardins, a French spiritual teacher who founded an ashram in his home country, stresses that we are all, deep down, already what we aspire to become, to be. Only an erroneous vision of ourselves (hence of others) prevents us from becoming aware of this fact. Too often, he stresses, we were not totally accepted as children. To respond to the wishes of our parents (who projected onto us the image of what they would have liked us to become), we tried to be other than what we were in our true identity. This created a split between the genuine us and the negative judgments we so often make about ourselves (often unconsciously). It is in a sense a refusal of our deep integrity, of what we are spontaneously, authentically. Focused on that demand, we hit a brick wall, metaphorically speaking.

Desjardins mentions that he has come to the conclusion that the most important message he can share today is that

> life loves us absolutely. Life created us and animates us. We are an expression of this superabundant life. God loves us unconditionally. If a rather severe religious education has convinced us that, here and now, in my sin, God cannot love me, this is a major error. God loves us, Reality loves us, the Life that animates us loves us.[1]

Blessing yourself is a precious way to learn to accept and to love yourself.

Get into a comfortable position, while at the same time staying perfectly alert. Make sure that you will not be disturbed and that you have some time. Then ponder for a while how much life loves you. Consider that there exists an infinite, tenderly encompassing

Love power that guides you and loves you unconditionally—so much that it joys over you with singing. Try to really feel this in your heart, not your head—this is anything but an intellectual exercise! Then, gently, start blessing yourself. Bless yourself in your perfect health and your goodness, your ability to forgive and love unconditionally—in every single area where you would like to progress. To start with, just take five to ten minutes a day, and you will garner a harvest of great abundance that will not only bless you but all those you encounter.

An intelligent love for ourselves, an authentic respect for who we are, is one of society's greatest needs. I write this as someone who has, for a great part of his life, worked with those who are down and out—most recently as a trainer for elderly unemployed and people on a minimal income. It is very difficult to bless others from the bottom of the heart (the only true kind of blessing) if we haven't started by loving and blessing ourselves. For how can we give to others what we refuse ourselves? We need to accept the wonderful, beautiful person, infinitely worthy of love that we are in our real being, our true self. Do you?

Each of us has exactly the same value and dignity as every single other person.

Each of us is *absolutely unique in time, space, and eternity*—in other words, in the now of human existence and in life eternal. There are no clones in God's universe!

Each of us has a unique role to play, our own special gift to make to the planet. Each of us needs to sing our song before continuing life in the spiritual form, which will be ours after death.

Have you sung your song? Have you made your gift?

Have you ever pondered the amazing fact that the infinite Love which governs the universe *needs* you—because an infinite being lacking even an atom, not to mention an individual like you, would be neither infinite, nor perfect, nor complete?

Let the following truth sink slowly into your consciousness: *I am absolutely unique. The Love which governs the universe* (which you can name Allah, Rama, the Source, God, whatever) *cherishes me completely. In Her eyes, I am infinitely precious.* Please, really ponder the meaning of these two words: *infinitely* and *precious.* What would you not do for someone who was infinitely precious to you? *And even if I do not yet feel this, I am totally one with this source of infinite, unlimited goodness.*

Why not start your morning meditation by simply allowing yourself to feel the strength, tenderness, gentleness, and intelligence of this infinite Love that surrounds you completely, from which you can never be separated, which is closer to you than your own thoughts? At each instant, this Love is silently whispering to you, "You are my dearly beloved expression in whom I am well pleased."

FORGIVING YOURSELF

Learn to forgive yourself completely and totally for all past mistakes.

Clean your slate! Loving and forgiving others starts by loving and forgiving ourselves. The most meaningful definition of true forgiveness (the concept of which has been highly misrepresented in our religious culture) I have ever come across is from Edith Stauffer in her book *Unconditional Love and Forgiveness.* She writes,

> *Forgiveness is a willingness to hold a certain attitude. It is a willingness to move forward. It is a willingness to be more comfortable and suffer less. It is a willingness to take responsibility*

for oneself and allow others to take responsibility for them-
selves. Forgiveness is a decision not to punish ourselves for the
wrongs of others or other circumstances. It is a decision to
re-enter the flow of love and life.

So, bless yourself in your true innocence, daily, for deep
down that is the ultimate truth of your being. Give up that self-
condemnation, that grudge, that regret or resentment, and let
yourself re-enter the flow of love and life. You can do it hour after
hour, again and again, until you discover the joy of running with
the stream rather than trying to push the river backwards or
sitting on the edge, woefully wishing you could flow with it!

You have the choice of the life you wish to lead, moment by
moment. And every minute, every thought, every gesture brings you
closer to or further from your aim. In every single present moment
you are preparing the kind of life you will live tomorrow, in two, ten,
twenty years from now—and even after what is called death.

The most important choices we make in life are not the dramatic turning points such as a change of career, the person we
marry, the country we emigrate to. The most important choices in
life are the thoughts and feelings we choose to entertain, moment
after moment, day after day. They shape our lives more surely than
any outward circumstance. So why not opt for an existence of
blessing—of blessing life moment after moment? After all, each
moment is the repository of infinite opportunities, ever renewed.

A lack of authentic self-love (which is completely different
from egoism and has no trace of selfishness) results nearly always
from a residue of thoughts of self-condemnation, which lurk in the
cave of the human ego, the mental realm. Guilt is the mafia of the
mind—do not let that mafia reign in your inner home! Complete

freedom is our spiritual heritage, and no one nor any teaching can deprive us of it.

And when we commit mistakes, we can know that the Divinity has *already* forgiven us, completely. Although this might seem too good to be true, divine forgiveness is prospective, and it covers all mistakes we could commit, even in the future. This is because our mistakes—any deviance from the great laws of the universe, some of which we have mentioned in this book—really constitute mistakes *against ourselves* and against our own happiness, even when they seem aimed at others.

For instance, to go against the law of harmony—expressed in the great teachings of spiritual wisdom since time immemorial and expressed in the major spiritual works of humanity—harms *us*, not the infinite intelligence that decreed these laws. This might be explained by saying that if Providence does not condemn, certain negative attitudes or behaviors we manifest can lead to a temporary self-exclusion from grace.

Let me give an example of how our transgression of fundamental spiritual and ethical laws of the universe constitutes a serious mistake against ourselves. I love thinking of the Ten Commandments as the Ten Promises. As a matter of fact, once I started thinking of them in that manner, it revolutionized my whole thinking about spiritual laws and these Commandments. They are powerful guidelines divine Love has given us for our own happiness. They include the promise "Thou shalt not commit adultery." In other words, if you are really aware of being a daughter/son of God, and if you are faithful to your highest sense of love, which means wanting the real good of your partner or of yourself, you will not even desire to have sexual escapades, because you know perfectly well that in so doing, you would imperil your own happiness.

This is exactly what happened to a couple who were good friends of mine. They had an extraordinary relationship, and the communication between them flowed beautifully and easily. Then, as the wife admitted to me, each had rather futile relationships outside the marriage. They did not last, but they were enough to break the magic of their relationship forever. They have not yet recovered from this break, which led to a divorce that was extremely tough on their two children.

Spiritually speaking, we are all still children. We need guidelines, a pedagogy to lead us on, to help us grow, until we have so completely internalized the caring intent of these laws that they one day become springboards to a higher freedom where there are no more laws, only the *infinitely creative spontaneity of love.*

Certain religious teachings based on fear have carefully avoided stressing the prospective nature of divine forgiveness, because the minute people become aware of the extraordinary fact of a Divinity which never condemns, fear-tinted teachings would have very little hold—if any—on their followers.

One of the reasons the parable of the Prodigal Son (Luke 15:11–32) has for centuries been one of the two or three favorite parables of the Christian tradition is that it is such a powerful metaphor for forgiveness. This parable tells the story of a son who wishes to leave the family home after having asked his father for his part of the inheritance.[2] He then goes abroad, where he squanders all his inheritance in wild living and ends up broke. Reduced to such extreme poverty that he envies the food of the pigs he is watching over, he decides to return home and ask his father for a job as a laborer on the family farm.

Never accepting the young man's departure, his father keeps an alert watch for his return. One day, he sees his son approaching home dressed in rags. He runs up to the boy and embraces him. (Most Bible commentators have not commented on this extraordinary fact of the father running toward the son, which was in complete contradiction to the Semitic customs in which a father would normally have considered such behavior totally at odds with the image of dignified poise and composure he was supposed to maintain.)

After the son condemns himself and his behavior, his father gives him a great big hug, orders a ring to be put on his finger (symbolizing oneness reinstated), replaces his rags with a white robe (the symbol of innocence and unconditional forgiveness), and organizes a major banquet in his honor. Once more, this goes completely against the grain of culture, where people are supposed to pay—often very dearly—for their mistakes.

This parable is not only a powerful symbol of our spiritual path but equally a representation of our progress hour after hour. At times, we are completely swallowed up by our social and human activity, to the extent of losing our spiritual bearings; the very next moment we awaken spiritually and find ourselves one with our source.

One of the most remarkable facts of this story is that the father does not have a single word of condemnation for this son who has squandered a good part of the family fortune by giving wild parties and running around with prostitutes. Not a single reprimand such as "Finally, you have come back to your good senses," or "This time, I will forgive you," or "Thank God your grandparents know nothing of what happened." Because the father is aware of the sincere remorse and repentance of his son (who realizes he has sinned, not against his father, but against his own happiness, the joy of a life lived in the omnipresence of Love), he gives a blanket pardon, offers his unconditional forgiveness without the slightest demand for some kind of atonement. "For three weeks, you will clean the pig sty" or even "No desserts and no outings for the next four months." Worse, from the point of view of traditional human morality, the father organizes a huge banquet to celebrate his son's return. Now, that's really going *too* far! Which is exactly what the elder brother claims.

The kind of religious thinking that loves to keep accounts—the one that keeps a huge ledger of debits and credits—is based on a conditional love, on retribution. And because deep down it refuses forgiveness, it *cannot* forgive itself. And it cannot forgive itself because it has never learned to love itself. This rigid, spindly, pathetic kind of thinking whose favorite pastime is nit-picking is deeply offended by the father's attitude. Unconditional, totally free love is not only incomprehensible for this kind of thinking, it is scandalized by it. In the parable, it is represented by the elder son, the image of stern virtue, who reproaches his father for not even letting him organize a small party with his orderly, decent friends, despite years of good behavior and hard work. And here comes his younger brother who has blown the family fortune in immoral behavior and reckless living and who is treated like a prince. Where will such laxity lead?! And I can understand that this apparent inequality of treatment is offensive to some, as it was to me when I harbored stern Calvinistic beliefs.[3]

This kind of religious thinking based on accounting is still very widespread. In fact, many of us harbor both brothers in our thinking! And it is only when one has understood the totally gratuitous nature of true forgiveness which only requests authentic repentance to clean the slate that one grasps the deeper sense of this parable.

FEELING INFINITE LOVE

Now I would like to propose that, if you feel burdened by images of an angry God or the like, you do a visualization exercise in which you see and especially feel yourself as the younger brother (or sister) in this parable. But first, become aware of the fact that any evil we commit, any harm we do or think, is a sin against ourselves, our own happiness and fulfillment, because in the long run the only way of expressing the wholeness of our divine being (which some call salvation) is to follow the major spiritual laws of the universe. (It is interesting to remember that in the Hebrew language, the original meaning of the verb *to sin* comes from archery and means "missing one's aim." In the English language, a similar etymology can be found in the verbs *trespass* and *transgress*, meaning "to step across a mark.") Be sure to have plenty of time and as much quiet as possible. Do this exercise when you are completely alone and sure not to be disturbed.

Feel yourself reaching the realization that going against any spiritual law is working against ourselves, our true fulfillment. Then see the loving father (or mother, if this has more meaning for you) running toward you and giving you a huge hug. Be aware of your astonishment when you realize he has not a single word of condemnation for you. See the light in his eyes—reflecting a love so radical in its absence of any conditions, so totally accepting of you as you are now, that it effaces any residue of self-condemnation you might have ever entertained. Feel him taking off your torn, smelly, dirty cloak and giving it to a servant, who immediately burns it in a nearby fire. Feel the white robe of pure silk slipping on your sore skin, this robe which represents your fundamental, ontological innocence—an innocence that constitutes the very essence of your true being, an innocence that has never known a so-called fall, because it never left the consciousness and omnipresence of infinite Love. (All this time, the ego, the deceptive little *i* that constantly requests pampering, has roamed and wandered through the mystifying and often dreary world of material appearances and empty social conventions, trying to deceive you into taking it for your true Self.)

Hear the father telling you, "I never saw you except as totally innocent, utterly guiltless. Only the little human ego left home. There is absolutely no condemnation. Your true Self never left my presence. What is happening is not really a return home but an awakening to your true identity, your true place. There is nothing in the whole universe that can separate you from me, infinite Love, the very substance of your being."

Complete this exercise by feeling the allness of infinite, ever-present Love, which fills every nook and cranny in the universe. Because of its allness, it cannot be invaded from the outside. (How could there be an outside to infinity?) It cannot be marred or deteriorate from the inside, because it is the cause and Creator of the tiniest particle. It is not going anywhere, because it fills all space. We truly are safe, totally and forever, in its omnipresence. Finally, take a moment to meditate on this truly amazing fact which I repeat because it is so vitally important: Love's forgiveness is prospective—it extends toward the future as well as effacing all the past, because in the consciousness of infinite Love, time does not exist; there is only the consciousness of perfect bliss in the ever-renewed present moment.

Every seeker on the spiritual path lives this parable many times a day. Sometimes we are the prodigal son or daughter: This happens each time our thought is caught in the snare of superficial appearances or negative emotions and thoughts. Sometimes we are the elder brother or sister, so engrossed in spiritual accounting practices that we forget that infinite Love makes a compulsory or servile attachment to such practices completely grotesque. ("Oh, I didn't do such-and-such a prayer today . . . I did not do my thirty minutes' meditation, or respect my fast . . . I did not read my sacred text X or Y, study the lesson, repeat my rosary or my sutra.") And sometimes we are the unconditionally forgiving mother or father.

Most people will find it useful to do this exercise more than once. If you are one of the very rare people who feel no trace of self-condemnation, do the exercise thinking of someone you know who could be helped by it.

A last comment on this parable: It is not the monopoly of any religion.[4] We could correctly say that it is not even a Christian parable (in the denominational sense of the word), as it was told by a wandering Jewish teacher long before the word *Christian* came into existence. It belongs to all religions and peoples. It is, in the noblest sense of the word, a mythological or symbolical representation of the human condition. *Anyone* can do the above visualization, be they Buddhist, Bahai, Muslim, Zoroastrian, Hindu, whatever.

As stressed in that beautiful book on the spiritual path, *A Course in Miracles*, the ultimate error of the human condition could well be separation, division, the belief of dualism. This is a favorite pastime of the ego—seeing a divided world: man and nature, male and female, races and nationalities, ideologies, classes, sects, good people, and bad people—the list of its labels is endless. Yet many great spiritual teachings of humanity insist time and again that *all is one*, and we are the expression of a life that transcends time, space, human existence, all beliefs of success and failure, of worth and worthlessness, and finally, death.

The more we bless from the heart, with a deep longing to see the good in all, the more these divisions will fall away and we will develop a gentle sense of the oneness of all life.

On Your Path to Blessing

*How much do you love yourself? How can
you love and accept yourself more fully?
What do you need to forgive yourself for?
If our thoughts are our most important decisions we make in life, how can you start
choosing more consciously?*

NOTES

1. Desjardins, Arnaud, "La vie nous aime, absolument, à chaque instant," *Terre du Ciel* magazine, Lyon, France, no. 33 (no date given).

2. So as to not burden the text, I have not written "father/mother" each time, but readers will remember it is an unstated assumption. Depending on the relationships of authority that existed in their family, some readers might prefer visualizing a mother who forgives rather than a father. Likewise, a son can also be replaced by a daughter. Adapt it to your own circumstances and to what speaks to you from the heart.

3. The monumental study by French historian Jean Delumeau, *Le péché et la peur au Moyen-Âge*, illustrates how the message of freedom of the gospels was distorted and replaced by a message of guilt and sin which created the foundations for a religion based on fear. Interested readers might continue with Jacques Ellul's *The Subversion of Christianity*, which describes the subversion of the Christian message in the early centuries. Ellul is one of the key French thinkers and writers of the postwar years.

4. One of the most remarkable presentations of the great spiritual teachings of humanity is the anthology by Aldous Huxley, *The Perennial Philosophy*.

13

BLESSING AS A SPIRITUAL PATH

Go after experience rather than knowledge. On account of pride,
knowledge may often deceive you, but this gentle, loving affection will
not deceive you. Knowledge tends to breed conceit, but love builds.
Knowledge is full of labor, but love, full of rest.
THE CLOUD OF UNKNOWING AND THE BOOK OF PRIVY COUNSELING

All through this book, I've encouraged you to be pragmatic. Practice blessing, for it is a practice, *only* a practice, and nothing but a practice. Nothing could be further removed, spiritually, from theory than the pursuit, art, joy, and path of blessing. It is the energy of the heart, of love, not of the mind or intellect. Knowledge often deceives, as the unknown English author of that gem of mystical literature *The Cloud of Unknowing and the Book of Privy Counseling* reminds us in the above epigraph. The gentle art, if practiced with sincerity and perseverance, will *never* let you down because it is based on unfailing spiritual laws. It will lead you into green pastures you never dreamed of. As in the case of the widow in the Old Testament story whose numerous empty pots are filled with oil from a single jar, blessing will turn the barren spaces of your existence into flowing waters of life. It can become a permanent spiritual practice that will transform your relationships—with people, nature, creatures of all kinds. You will discover the beauty of your enemies, and drudgery will be transformed into music.

Knowledge, as the author of *The Book of Privy Counseling* comments, is full of labor (if it remains an intellectual pursuit, I would add, as opposed to truly liberating knowledge, which is a deep and spontaneous spiritual understanding, the gift of grace). Blessing, at least after the initial learning, and often right from the start, is full of rest. In the midst of the worst tempest, when your lifeboat is rocking wildly, it will calm the waves and you will discover a deep, deep repose.

The art of blessing can become a privileged means of spiritual growth. You'll see in this chapter that blessing incorporates key elements of some of the most cherished spiritual practices of the major spiritual paths of humanity.

GOOD-BYE, LITTLE EGO!

I have found that blessing is a glorious way to shake off that nagging, constant burden we call the ego. Indeed, for many spiritual teachings, the death of the human ego is the key turning point of the spiritual path. In one of the most powerful brief spiritual autobiographies I have ever read, at the end of his book *Power versus Force: The Hidden Determinants of Human Behavior*, Dr. David R. Hawkins states, "The person I had been no longer existed. There was no personal self or ego, only an infinite Presence of such unlimited Power that it was all there was. The Presence replaced what had been 'me.'"

Some profound passages on the death of the ego can be found in the writings of the Sufi mystic Rumi:[1]

Make a journey from self to Self, oh friend. . . . Purify yourself from the attributes of self, so that you may see your own pure essence! . . . I have become senseless, I have fallen into selflessness—in absolute selflessness, how joyful I am with Self! . . . No one will find his way to the Court of Magnificence until he is annihilated.

The most beautiful expression of this death of the ego or little i that I have come across is in the writings of the great Indian teacher Sri Aurobindo, who stated,

the liberated man . . . has abandoned all attachment to the fruits of his works, and where one does not work for the fruit, but solely as an impersonal instrument of the Master of works, desire can find no place, not even the desire to serve success-fully—for the fruit is the Lord's and determined by him and not by personal will and effort,—or to serve with credit to the Master's satisfaction. For the real doer is the Lord Himself."

Practicing constant blessing deprives the ego of the time or energy to mull over its self-created problems, air its fears or desires, pander to self-centeredness—in other words, to strut around saying "i . . . i . . . i . . ." ad nauseam. It will help erode the little ego to such wafer-like unreality that it will one day suddenly deflate into its native nothingness.

THE USE OF BLESSING AS A SPIRITUAL AFFIRMATION OR MANTRA

The art of blessing has considerable affinity with a broad spectrum of practices that help those on the spiritual path constantly re-center their thinking on the divine. One of the privileged ways of doing this in the Hindu tradition is the use of a mantra. A mantra is a short statement, sometimes just a few words or even one word, constantly repeated throughout the day. A similar practice is frequent in the tradition of the Eastern Orthodox churches and medieval spirituality, as exemplified by numerous other writings, including this passage from *The Cloud of Unknowing*: "If you want to gather all your desire into one simple word that the mind can retain, choose a short word rather than a long one. A one syllable word such as 'God' or 'love' is best. But choose one that is meaningful to you. Then fix it in your mind so that it will remain there come what may."

The risk with such practices is that they can become unthinkingly mechanical. Such a risk, although small, is much less with blessing, which, because it is usually uttered in response to a specific situation, always needs to be something fresh.

As a matter of fact, this is one of the extraordinary aspects of this practice: You can do it dozens, even hundreds of times in a day, and it can stay as fresh the 113th time when you return home at midnight as at the start of the day. It is just like a spring: Have you ever heard of a spring turning stale or tasteless after a particularly long day of activity, catering to hundreds of thirsty passersby on an especially hot summer day? Of course not. Blessing is a spring, and the spring is our heart, and our heart never need grow old or tired. At eighty, it can stay as intact, fresh, and enthusiastic as at fifteen.

Above all, this constant centering and resting of the mind on the kingdom within will, little by little, bring with it that peace which passeth all understanding.

Being Present to the Present Moment

Few practices are more central to living a spiritually centered life—and simply living—than the art of living in the present moment.[2] We live in societies where most people are either living in the past with regret, resentment, or remorse or in the future with hopes, fears, ambitions, dreams, and plans of all sorts. Yet we can only *live*, I mean *really* live, in the present moment. This awareness is especially strong in the Buddhist tradition. It is a major theme of the writings of the well-known Buddhist teacher Thich Nhat Hanh and of the beautiful book on meditation by John Kabat-Zinn, *Mindfulness Meditation for Everyday Life*. And of course it is also a central theme of Eckhart Tolle's *The Power of Now*.

Blessing whatever you do is a fresh, wonderful way of staying centered, of being present to the present—the present moment, present place and environment, present activity, present circumstances—the bus you are on, the subway you travel in, the meal you eat, the person to whom you speak, the child with whom you play (including the one inside you), the people with whom you work, and so on.

For a person who is unemployed, for instance, blessing will open up extraordinary employment opportunities. As you bless others, the very practice could open doors that could ultimately lead to gainful employment. The possibilities are limitless.

And why not bless every payment you make—including, yes, your taxes! Have you ever thought of the fact that every time you make a payment, you represent the abundance of the universe for someone? Most of us enjoy receiving money—be it our paycheck, a gift, an unexpected windfall, whatever. So why not make giving money something of equal enjoyment as receiving it? Only the intellect separates giving from receiving, because it desperately needs to label everything and fit all experiences into neat little cubbyholes! In reality, both are expressions of the infinite abundance of good in the universe. Hence they are, in fact, exactly the same thing.

The more you get into the gentle art of blessing, the more you will find meaningful ways to express it. For instance, every time I mail letters, I bless them on their errand of communication, trusting the person receiving it will feel better for it. A friend of mine stands next to his bed the minute he gets up and blesses his wife as she sleeps (he is an early riser). He sends her blessings of protection for the day, he blesses her in her innocence, her perfect health, above all her divinity and her perfection. "And having gotten off to such a good start, I send her blessings all through the day," he adds.

If you are a teacher, for instance, why not get to class early and bless each of the children, thinking of them by name and blessing each of them in a specific way? Miracles will happen. Just try. A friend of mine who is an adult trainer blesses all the people who take his courses before he even meets them. If you are a farmer, why not bless your cows, geese and chicken, fields and nature?

I am far from the goal of constant blessing. As mentioned in the introduction to this book, I am still very much a beginner on the spiritual path. But I have learned that blessing is an exciting and highly effective way to be fully present in every moment.

The Karma Yoga of Blessing

Karma yoga is a spiritual teaching found in the Bhagavad Gita, one of the holy scriptures of Hinduism. It recommends a complete detachment of the self from our action—a concept that has also been expressed by other spiritual writers, for example Isaiah's statement,

"Lord, thou wilt ordain peace for us: for thou also has wrought all our works in us" (Isaiah 26:12). This is a perfect summary of karma yoga.

Among the eight key teachings of karma yoga, three are particularly relevant to the art of blessing:

1. **Do not desire any of the fruits of your action.**
   In other words, you become totally detached from the benefits of what you are doing—for instance, as you bless people you meet in the street whom you might never meet again. Because you will never see the results of your silent, unselfed blessings, these become a significant step toward inner liberation. You receive not the slightest expression of praise or gratitude for these silent blessings, which is one of the most wonderful dimensions of blessing. This constant selfless giving puts the ego—which normally constantly clamors for recognition—on a radical slimming diet! This unending, daily, hour-after-hour selfless blessing of others *will create in you a deep desire for the authentic, total happiness of every single creature*, especially if you include the environment, plants, and animals in your blessings.

   "The only work that spiritually purifies is that which is done without personal motives, without desire for fame or public recognition or worldly greatness, without insistence on one's mental motives ... done for the sake of the Divine alone and at the command of the divine," wrote Aurobindo. This is a perfect definition of true blessing.

2. **Act without any attachment to the action itself.**
   In the practice of blessing, we get to a point where we bless for the sheer joy of blessing, as a silent perfume

153

we send forth, a silent song. At some moment, the little ego will, of course, attempt to put on its self-important airs (e.g., "How virtuous I am to bless everyone like this" and similar squeaks of deluded vanity) but we just let them slide like water off a duck's back. You will not be tricked by these pathetic maneuvers. You will remember that a song is absolutely nothing of itself; it is totally dependent on the singer. It has absolutely no existence in and of itself at any time. It is the pure effect of the divine cause.

Eventually you will have no more attachment to the act of blessing than to your own heartbeat—and spiritually speaking, blessing is the heartbeat of the soul. Blessing becomes as natural as breathing, and as effortless.

3. **Consider not yourself as the cause or source of action.**
The next natural step toward becoming a simple witness of life in action is to become aware of the fact that because there is only one infinite, true cause in the universe—infinite, unconditional Love, the source of all good—we are not the cause of the blessing, any more than the song or the edelweiss are the cause of their own beauty and harmony. In utter awe, we observe Love acting *as* us (rather than *through* us). The apostle Paul wrote in a moment of deep mystical intuition, "Yet not I, but Christ liveth in me" (Galatians 2:20). Here Christ is to be understood in the sense of divine life, truth, and love in action—through and as our blessings—to heal the world.

Like a lever, the simplest tools are sometimes the most efficient and powerful ones. Such is this gentle art.

IT IS THE SPIRIT THAT COUNTS

In one of those wonderful folk tales, poetry master Leo Tolstoy tells the story of an orthodox bishop who is traveling on the Black Sea. During the trip, he hears of an island inhabited by three hermits. He expresses the desire to visit them. As at that time people did not need to cling to tight travel schedules, the captain stops the ship close to the island, and the bishop, on a smaller boat, is taken there. He meets the three hermits and tells them that, as their bishop, he wishes to see what he could teach them. He asks them how they pray. "We pray in this way," replied the hermits. "Three are ye, three are we, have mercy upon us."

The bishop comments that they have evidently heard of the Trinity. "I see you wish to please the Lord, but you do not know how to serve Him. That is not the way to pray; but listen to me, and I will teach you." He then sets forth to teach them the Lord's Prayer. He spends the whole day with them, getting them to repeat it time and again, and only when, at the end of the day, he is assured that they are able to pray it correctly, does he leave. On the little boat taking him back to the ship, he hears the three voices diligently repeating the Lord's Prayer.

In the evening, alone on the bridge, the bishop is meditating. Suddenly, he sees something white and shining on the sea, but it is neither boat, bird, nor fish. He approaches the helmsman. Together they finally discern what it is: the three hermits running upon the water, gray beards shining and effortlessly catching up with the moving ship. The steersman, in terror, lets go of the helm. When they catch up to the ship, the hermits cry to the stunned bishop, "We have forgotten your teaching, servant of God. As long as we kept repeating it, we remembered, but when we stopped saying it for a time, a word dropped out, and now it has all gone to pieces. . . . Teach us again."

Crossing himself, the bishop leans over the ship's side and cries out, "Your own prayer will reach the Lord, men of God. It is not for me to teach you. Pray for us sinners." And he bows very low in front of the three old hermits as they turn back across the sea. And till daybreak, a light shone on the spot where they had been.

As Tolstoy's story suggests with humor, it is the spirit that counts, not the form. May that reassure anyone who wishes to start blessing. And without guaranteeing that the joyful practice of this art will enable you to immediately walk on water, I hope, dear reader, that you have glimpsed through these pages that this approach to life, situations, and people makes available to any sincere person invaluable treasures of peace, contentment, compassion, and especially healing.

A SPIRIT THAT IS AWARE CAN HEAL

Above everything else, our world cries out for healing: A healing of the growing wounds wrought by an economic system in which the rich get richer and the poor poorer to an extent unparalleled in human history. (According to UN statistics, 368 billionaires very literally sit on wealth equivalent to the income of 45 percent of the world's population, while half the world's population lives on two dollars a day or less.) A healing of ethnic, religious, political, national, class, and other rifts of all sorts. The healing of major social evils like drugs, criminality, alcoholism, and family, neighborhood, and media violence. The physical healing of major pandemics like tuberculosis and malaria (again on the upswing),

AIDS, and leprosy, to mention but a few. The healing of hunger on an unprecedented scale—tens of thousands die of hunger every day, many of them children. The healing of hundreds of millions worldwide who are excluded from the economic system through unemployment. The healing of our environment which, despite significant improvements in some areas, is giving serious warnings of major crises ahead. The healing of human relations in general, in societies where people are running up ladders faster and faster without even wondering if they have put their ladders against the right wall or if they are running in the right direction. And the urgent healing of child prostitution and sexual exploitation, which is the greatest affront to human dignity. (It is estimated that two million children are drawn into the commercial sex trade every year.) The list could cover pages.

No, there are no ivory towers available for the authentic spiritual healers we can all become once we have just started glimpsing the healing power of blessing. And yes, you can start becoming a spiritual healer in the middle of this page: you could, for instance, put the book down and spend ten minutes blessing the three persons you dislike most on the planet (be they neighbors or faraway dictators), or blessing children living in ghettos, or the inmates of the local jail. Blessing is one field where the risk of redundancy or unemployment is absolutely nil!

If our state of consciousness contributes to a great extent to the creation of our reality and the very experiences we encounter, then a spirit that is aware and alert, and a heart that is at peace, are sorely needed for the healing of many of these ills. And the gentle art of blessing helps at all times to keep an alert mind and spirit, and a compassionate, serene heart.

BLESSING CENTERS YOUR SPIRIT

Another fruit of the practice of blessing is that it will create for you a space of stability in a world of constant change and seemingly growing confusion. Those who have lived through the past fifty years or so have experienced one of the greatest mental upheavals of human history: Whereas stability used to be the norm and change the exception, we now live in a world where *change is the norm and stability the exception*. Everything changes, everywhere, in all fields, at top speed, at the same time. The wheels of history are turning faster and faster.

In addition to that, as Nobel Prize winner Arno Penzias has observed, we are the first generation in history during which knowledge will be renewed more than once in a generation, meaning that scientific theories and observations are changing so rapidly that in thirty years people might hear very different explanations from what we hear now. What happens to people who experience such avalanches of change in societies where behavioral norms are disappearing in many areas?

Well, blessing will help you find your center at the hub of the wheel, which stays still however fast the wheel turns. The art of blessing will anchor you in a transcendental dimension of divine omnipresence which little by little will transform your whole life. And to quote the metaphor of Swiss writer Charles-Ferdinand Ramuz, it is the tree with the deepest roots which can extend its branches the furthest. "And the leaves of the tree were for the healing of the nations," as a verse from the Bible states (Revelation 22:2). You can become that tree, and every one of your leaves (blessings) an instrument of healing.

If one person blessing has the power to heal, what amazing things could happen when people join together to bless? In early 2009, a friend and I launched a healing experiment with the potential to expand rapidly: Blessing Circles. Our vision for the Blessing Circles is a caregiving group committed to world healing (in the spirit of the description of the real fast in Isaiah 58), deep compassion, unconditional love, total respect, and nonjudgment, regardless of where members are on their spiritual journey. These Blessing Circles will help participants to

❧ enhance the development of consciousness and healing

❧ be part of a dynamic, thriving, spiritually based lay group (meaning not attached to any specific religious structure, dogma, or movement, even if some individual members are members of such groups and organizations)

❧ contribute meaningfully to the solution of individual, community, and world problems through the practice of blessing

❧ provide a warm, friendly, supportive, and relaxed circle setting to encourage the mutual spiritual growth of the participants

If this idea appeals to you, please see the multilingual website *www.ourblessingcircles.com*, where you can take part in the Blessing Circles movement.

BE A SENDER OF BLESSINGS

Blessing is not a panacea, by any means, still less a magic wand. You might need years of joyful, persevering practice before discovering its power and all its ramifications. The well of our inner garden is infinite in its depth and freshness, and we will drink the waters thereof to the extent that we cultivate its proximity and visit it often—in meditation, in prayer, in blessing, and above all, in *living* love.

"Many little streams make the great Zambezi," says a proverb from Zimbabwe. Thousands of people who, each in their own corner, unpretentiously bless those around them, truly help to create a better world. More is needed, of course—much more. But it is a simple healing step every single person can take, be you bedridden, in prison (and there are many ways of being imprisoned), washing the dishes, walking along the street.

In his "Song of the Open Road," Walt Whitman wrote,

Afoot and light-hearted, I take to the open road,
Healthy, free, the world before me,
The long brown path before me, leading wherever I choose.

Why not walk that path while blessing? It *will* help make the journey lighthearted and free.

The impact of these blessings might be compared to the story (which exists in many versions) of the old lady by the sea. A particularly violent storm threw millions of starfish on the beach. The old lady is throwing them back into the sea, one by one. A person passing by sees her and asks her what on earth she is doing. "There are millions and millions of them! What do you hope to achieve? They are all going to die." The old lady takes a starfish which she throws with special concentration and vitality into the sea, and with a joyful glint in her beautiful blue eyes exclaims, "For *this* one, it made all the difference."

One single blessing, friend, can make all the difference.

Each blessing you send into the universe is like a star which lights up, somewhere. It might sound amazing, but each felt, authentic blessing is an act of life which reverberates to the ultimate reaches of the universe and echoes to the end of time.

Let us be senders of blessings. Then truly shall we be children of the light.

Dear reader friend, may your life overflow with blessings!

I promise you that if you make blessing into a way of life, the following lines from the book of Isaiah (55:12) will become true for you:

> *For ye shall go out with joy,*
> *and be led forth with peace:*
> *The mountains and the hills*
> *shall break forth before you into singing,*
> *and all the trees of the field*
> *shall clap their hands.*

Thank you for existing. You are a blessing to our precious little planet and to all of us.

PIERRE PRADERVAND

NOTES

1. The vision of many mystics and the inner garden of the Sufis is also shared by a transpersonal school of psychology called psychosynthesis, founded by the Italian psychiatrist Roberto Assagioli. Piero Ferrucci, in *What We May Be*, summarizes this school of thought.

2. For more on the "centering" process, see *The Miracle of Mindfulness*; *The Long Road to Joy*; and *Present Moment Wonderful Moment*, all by Thich Nhat Hanh.

BLESSINGS FOR EVERYDAY LIFE

I offer the blessings that follow just to stimulate your imagination—they in no way pretend to be models, although you may wish to use them in your daily life. Some are blessings for a group of persons; most are blessings a person in a given profession might wish to use to prepare their day.

For instance, if you are not too happy about the manner in which your local newspaper, radio, or TV station (or any other medium) covers events, you can write to them. You might also try blessing them. And if you bless them first for a few weeks and then write a letter, there is a good possibility the letter will not only be much better written but will be better accepted, because you have sent your white thought-birds (see chapter 4) in advance to prepare your way.

A BLESSING FOR JOURNALISTS

I bless all journalists (or the journalists of [name of station or newspaper/magazine]) in their great love for and responsiveness to truth, and their sensitivity to beauty and goodness. I bless them in their ability to avoid being manipulated into reporting trivia or hiding truth. They denounce evil only to correct it. I bless them in the complete integrity of their being, which leads them to avoid all cheap sensationalism and offensive probing of people's personal lives. I joyfully bless them in their constant ability to report with exactitude, integrity, and total fairness on all they are requested to present to their readers (listeners, viewers) and to avoid all pressures to dilute their high standards of truth for reasons of expediency, economic, or other.

A reminder: Blessing works on the level of invisible spiritual reality, not what appears to be happening on the level of material events. To material eyes, the journalists you are blessing may appear as totally unscrupulous, amoral profiteers who have only one concern: money and ego. That's the very reason you are blessing them: to help them access that space of pristine integrity and goodness, of unfailing compassion and tender caring, of constant striving for their highest sense of truth which exists deep inside all individuals, albeit they are often not aware of it.

A TAXI DRIVER'S BLESSING FOR THE DAY

Spirit of truth and love, I bless this day for all the goodness it already includes. I bless this cab as a rolling temple of Thy presence. I bless the roads I shall travel on, and all those whose paths I cross. I bless all people who enter this cab. I bless them in their coming and their going, in their perfect path, in their guidance and sense of direction.

I bless the space of this cab, that all who enter it may find therein peace and a moment's haven from the pressures of life. I bless myself in my patience, humor, and joy, that I may uplift the downhearted, console the sad, rejoice with those who rejoice, and be for each one the mirror of the infinite Mother-Love's caring for them.

I bless myself in my calm, that I may stay poised in the stress of urban traffic, smile at those who curse me, and end the day with a song in my heart and cash sufficient to cover all my needed expenses.

Blessing for a Couple Getting Married

This blessing could be said at the same time by both partners facing each other. It could also be said by a friend, in which case the "us"/"our" would be replaced by "you"/"your." (It is adapted from the marriage vows Elly and I made to each other.)

I bless us in our striving to seek each other's real good above all else, for that is our highest understanding of true love.

We will uphold each other's every effort to be our truest, most authentic self, wherever that may lead, and in every way to forward our mutual spiritual growth.

We will accompany each other without ever possessing each other.

My abundance shall be your supply, just as my need will be your opportunity to share your abundance.

I bless us in creating a rhythm of living where there is always space for inner listening, and to accept only those structures that help us grow, but never become barriers or crutches.

Together, we will choose the spirit of adventure rather than the false security of material comfort, trusting on our Father-Mother who clothes the lilies of the valley to give us our daily bread—in abundance, that we may share this divine wealth with all.

When your highest visions astonish me, I will listen rather than object, and if life's trials cause you to stumble or fall, I will put your hand in God's, where it will always meet mine. And this you will do for me.

For our greatest blessing is the assurance that, in the words of the apostle Paul (Romans 8:38–39), "neither death, nor life, nor angels, nor principalities, nor powers, nor things present, nor things to come, nor height, nor depth, nor any other creature, shall be able to separate us from the love of God"—or from each other.

And this love is the ultimate weave of the seamless garment of our oneness.

BLESSING FOR A NURSE

I bless this day as a series of ever-renewed opportunities to serve with love. May each of the leaves of my tree be for the healing of every individual I encounter. I especially bless and rejoice in the opportunities:

🌿 to do things well rather than carelessly or in a hurry

🌿 to smile rather than scowl or appear indifferent

🌿 to express love's tender interest to all those I meet

🌿 to pause and listen rather than rush on to the next task

I bless the hospital (doctor's practice) as a temple of love governed by a true spirit of service.

I bless the personnel in their diligence, humor, and good-naturedness.

I bless the doctors in their authentic listening, deep caring, and true compassion, their wisdom in identifying right treatments, and their openness to accepting that healing may come from many sources, including prayer.

I bless all patients in their courage, steadfastness, trust, light spirits, and their ability to strengthen their immune system by expressing a generous portion of one of the best medicines around—laughter.

And finally, I bless myself in my unruffled poise and serenity, my joy and my professional competence. May the fount of unconditional love, which is the essence of my true being, pour freely on all, including Thy humble servant.

PRISON INMATES' AND GUARDS' BLESSING

This blessing has been used by inmates on death row in Texas.

I bless this place of detention that despite locked doors and bars, its inmates may discover the freedom within.

I bless the inmates:

🌿 in their desire and ability to forgive, including themselves when needed

🌿 in their steadfastness, hope, and patience when days drag on

🌿 in their ability to summon from the depths of their true selves the supreme ability to return good for evil

🌿 in their unwavering trust in divine justice which ultimately wins and rights all wrongs—including those of a human penal system with its imperfections

❧ in their capacity to find bodily rest and peace despite the strain of prison conditions and, for many, their starved sexuality.

I bless the guards in their desire to treat inmates as fellow human beings, to look through the penal label to the soul hungering for brotherhood and sisterhood, to be generous and to apply the spirit of the rules rather than the letter.

I bless the inmates that they may unite with that space of integrity deep down inside them which has never been touched by error, fear, hatred, darkness, or lack of any sort, and rekindle the flame of their true being, which always remains pure, generous, and upright.

I bless all the prison personnel in their ability to do a challenging job in a spirit of service and deep compassion.

And finally, I bless the citizens of this country. May they understand that as long as any one of them is behind bars, a part of themselves is there too, and that by keeping certain inmates in conditions of detention that deny human dignity, they are denying the divine in themselves and the invisible spiritual oneness of all human beings.

A Blessing for Parents

We bless ourselves in this sacred trust of raising children and our ability to meet all challenges as they arise.

We bless the garden of our home in its ability to produce strong and beautiful plants from the rich soil of tested values which constitute the true nourishment of our children.

We bless Thee, Mother-Father God, for the sacred privilege of raising these divine children of the stars. May their light shine ever brighter, and may we and all others be receptive to their brilliance.

We bless ourselves in our ability to understand the incredible challenges of growing up in today's world. We bless our whole family in our ability to express boundless patience and unconditional love toward each other.

We bless ourselves in our wise transmission to our children of the inner sense of integrity that will enable them to resist undue peer pressure—be it sex, drugs, popularity, clothing, or drinking—with grace and humor, and be loved all the more for it.

We bless ourselves in our ability to share with our offspring that true wealth has little if anything to do with material possessions and a great deal to do with qualities such as love, compassion, and giving. May we express such qualities so unselfconsciously that our children will reflect them too.

Finally, we bless ourselves in our ability to stick together as a family through thick and thin, to do unto others as we would have them do unto us, and to be open to the world's problems and any heart in need.

A Blessing for Politicians

This blessing can, of course, be adapted to a local politician.

I bless the politicians of _____ in their highest sense of integrity, ability to put public service before personal gain, and aim for lasting long-term solutions rather than immediate political gains.

I bless them in their ability to resist undue pressure from lobbies of all sorts, and to manifest courage and moral rectitude rather than bend to expediency.

A RETAIL/SERVICE INDUSTRY EMPLOYEE'S BLESSING

I bless this day and the countless opportunities for service it offers.

I bless myself in my ability to do my best at all times, to work diligently and serenely, to manifest utmost patience and grace with irate or impatient customers, and to offer the precious gift of a smile to all those I encounter.

I bless the quality of my service, in its efficiency, cleanliness, and joy.

I bless myself in my strength, my tireless good humor, and my competence.

I bless the shop (café, restaurant, supermarket, bar, snack) where I work as a temple of Love's presence. May I reflect that presence at all times in unselfconscious goodness toward all, in my ability to lift the downhearted with a kind word or a smile, and in the gracefulness of my service.

Shine through me, and may I so reflect Thee so that all those I encounter may no longer see me, but only, only Thee, Thou infinite One.

A BLESSING FOR TEACHERS

I bless this day and the endless opportunities it offers me to share wisdom and truth, to extend compassion and understanding, to manifest patience and love toward all the students entrusted to my care.

I bless myself in my willingness to assume full responsibility—the ability to respond with creativity and love—for any situation that develops in the classroom, to handle tensions nonviolently, and to generate productive relationships with parents and staff alike.

I bless my ability to discern the divine and the good in every child/student, however contrary the outward appearance, to manifest steadfast poise and unruffled calm whatever the threats to discipline and orderly discussion in the classroom.

I bless the students in their desire to learn and progress, in their capacity to contribute positively to the atmosphere of the class, to cooperate with and help fellow classmates, and to resist peer and other pressures which would influence them toward absorbing drugs of any kind.

Above all, I bless myself in my ability to produce exciting courses that stretch students' intellect, strengthen their sense of values and morality, and develop their highest sense of vision, world citizenship, and authentic desire to be of service to their community and all humanity.

BLESSINGS FOR A FEW WORLD SITUATIONS

Lynne McTaggart, in her pioneering study The Intention Experiment *shows the extraordinary power of people's united intention for change. Below you will find blessings for four world problems that will hopefully inspire you, dear reader, to develop your own blessings for situations of concern to you.*

I am a great believer in the philosophy of many droplets filling oceans, expressed so beautifully by William James, who stated, I am done with great things and big things, great institutions and big success, and I am for those tiny, molecular moral forces that work from individual to individual, creeping through the crannies of the world like so many rootlets, or like the capillary oozing of the water, yet which, if you give them time, will rend the hardest monuments of man's pride.

A BLESSING FOR TERRORISTS

I bless those who are tempted to commit terrorist acts, whether out of despair, hatred, fear, lust for power, or any other tormented human motive.

I bless them in their integrity, that they may discover that the wholeness in themselves cannot be reached at the cost of the wholeness of others.

I bless them in their realization that love is the ultimate law governing the universe and mankind, and that their deepest honest longings can only be reached through the law of love.

I bless them in their awareness that, deep down, they are children of the light, and that terrorist schemes are but an inversion of the light with no true cause, substance, or law behind them.

I bless them in their understanding that the darkness they see or imagine can only be dispelled by light, not by more darkness.

I bless them in their unlimited goodness, kindness, compassion, and caring, which is waiting within to be kindled and brought to full fruition.

I bless them in their grasp of the law of right returns, that they may understand that the good or evil they do to another, they ultimately do unto themselves.

I bless them in their hunger and thirst for righteousness, that it may be fulfilled.

I bless them that any sense of lack they feel may be healed by a clearer consciousness of infinite abundance now; that any restlessness may give way to Thy peace; that any feeling of insecurity with its attendant aggressiveness or fear may be healed by the sense of Thy comforting presence; that any sense of separation, clanish-ness, and loneliness may be assuaged by the understanding that we are all one.

And I bless myself in my awareness that divine Love sees no ter-rorists, only its perfect reflection, and that this same consciousness can be mine as I understand that behind the veil of appearances, all men and women have one Mind, the divine Mind.

A BLESSING FOR LEADERS OF THE ECONOMY AND BUSINESS

The major economic and financial challenges the world is facing as this revised edition of The Gentle Art of Blessing *is underway have compelled me to add this blessing for those in positions of responsibility in this field.*

I bless those with major responsibilities in the economic and business fields.

I bless them in their spirit of ethical service, that they may offer useful quality products and services.

I bless them in their understanding of the law of right returns, so they may manifest the deep comprehension that what they give shall return to them, be it in relations with employees, clients, the public, or nature.

I bless them in their fundamental integrity expressed in the honesty of all the contracts and deals they make and the value of all they put on the market.

I bless them that their fear of lack may be effaced by a deep grasp of the infinite abundance of the universe and that true wealth is in ideas and values rather than things and money.

I bless them in their deep understanding that the economy ultimately exists to increase human well-being, that they may see money as a means, not an end.

I bless them in their grasping of the fact that only a win-win approach in all areas can possibly bring long-term harmony for all concerned, and that what blesses one, blesses all, and vice versa.

Finally, I bless them in their vision of an economy where quality and sometimes smallness is more important than quantity and size, and lived values override the bottom line.

And I bless myself in the realization that with every purchase I make, I am voting for a certain kind of world, that I may better live my beliefs in the choices I make every day.

A Blessing for Street Children and Children Forced into Prostitution

One of the major scandals of today is that in a world that has the ample possibility of providing the basic needs for all, tens of millions of children, sometimes as young as four years old, roam the streets, sleeping under bridges, in garbage dumps, and in cellars, if not on the open street. An estimated two million of them have to sell their bodies and their innocence so they and sometimes their families may eat. They are forced into prostitution against their will, often as the result of the abject poverty of their families.

From the deepest wellspring of my heart, I bless street children worldwide in their peace and rest.

I bless them in their deep sense of self-worth and self-respect, that they may transcend the numerous obstacles of which they are victims.

I bless them in the God-given creativity that resides in each one of them, that they may find their right place in society despite all obstacles.

I bless them in their inner beauty and light that shines in them whatever their appearences.

I bless them in their sense of abundance, that they may transcend all socially imposed beliefs of lack.

I bless the innumerable children who have been reduced to selling their bodies, that their innate innocence and purity may never be dimmed.

I bless them in their perfect health, that they may not be victims of AIDS or other sexually transmitted diseases.

I bless them in their consciousness of their divine nature, that it may efface any sense of self-condemnation, despair, fear, or powerlessness.

I bless them when they walk in the valley of the shadow of death. May they feel that Thy rod and Thy staff comfort and protect them.

I bless them in their infinite opportunity, that they may break free from this slavery and one day walk upright and free as useful citizens of their societies.

I bless the adults who use these children, that they may become aware of the depth of their wrongdoing and be led to repentance and reparation.

And finally, I bless myself that I may refuse to indulge in thought or in deed in the sensuality that reinforces the very existence of this exploitation.

A BLESSING FOR THE UNITED NATIONS

We live in a world that functions, in terms of communications, finances, geography, and so on, as a unified structure, with hundreds of millions of tourists, refugees, and migrants criss-crossing frontiers every year. However, legally and territorially, we are divided into over two hundred nations and territories. It is essential for our survival as a species that our nations become partners in an efficient global organization to protect human rights and the world's commons.

I bless the United Nations as a positive meeting ground for all nations.

I bless the UN in its ability to foster authentic dialogue between nations.

I bless the UN in its essential role as mediator in conflict, and I bless its peacekeeping forces that they may rise to the challenge of their often highly demanding task.

I bless the numerous specialized UN agencies in their task of developing and delivering international solutions to pressing world problems—in the fields of health, environment, employment, development, communications, the weather, finance, and many others.

I bless the personnel of the United Nations that they may develop a true sense of being world servants and a deep commitment to the goals of the UN.

I bless the UN as a promoter and defender of human rights worldwide that through an awareness of these rights we may develop a keener sense of our dignity and worth.

I bless our nations and governments in their recognition of our common destiny and their readiness to let go of nationalistic reflexes in favor of forwarding our ultimate destiny—which is oneness.

I bless the citizens of the world we all are in our ability to support the vision of a win-win world incarnated by the UN ideals essential to humankind's survival.

A BLESSING FOR YOURSELF

It is fitting that the last blessing in this book be for yourself, given in the spirit of Zephaniah 3:17.

Infinite Mother-Love, I bless myself as the smile of Thy great Love, as the song of Thine infinite goodness, as the stream of Thy refreshing Truth.

I bless myself in the discernment that enables me to realize that I am a stream, a song, a smile to all those I meet—as they are for me.

I bless myself in my guiltless innocence, in my full joy that none can rob or erode.

I bless myself in my peace that is as deep as the ocean and as calm as the lake at dusk.

Use and reinvent this blessing every day, adding the qualities you especially wish to express—patience, intelligence, purity, strength, humor, whatever. Remember that as the reflection, the smile of God, you already have these qualities as a part of you. They do not have to be added on, but simply unveiled.

Enjoy the unveiling, dear friend. It will become the greatest discovery in your existence.

EPILOGUE: BLESSING—
A PRACTICE THAT HEALS

For many years, I have been receiving letters, phone calls, and emails from all around the world on the healing impact of blessing. I'd like to share some of the correspondence I've received about the impact of blessing in everyday life. For reasons of confidentiality, I have occasionally changed the first names.

In October 2005, I gave a talk on spirituality and, the next day, ran a workshop on blessing at the College of Psychic Studies in London. During the talk, I briefly mentioned the practice of blessing. A participant, an Irish woman, went home on the subway, where she struck up a conversation with a young man. They got on so well they continued talking on a bench at the station where they both got off. He saw a friend and hailed him over. The friend sat on the other side of the lady. A moment later, she left to go home. After a few steps, she realized the second young man had stolen her purse. Instead of screaming or making a scandal of some sort, she told herself, "Well, if this blessing Pierre talked about works, I simply need to bless him." She did that for a few seconds and then turned around; the young pickpocket was coming toward her with her purse in his hand.

She opened the workshop the next day by telling this story—what a golden gift she made to all participants!

My African friend from the Sahel, Mahmoudou Kassambara (whom I quoted at the beginning of this book), has had his life completely transformed by the practice of blessing. It has become a second nature to him, to the extent that I told him he had become my teacher in the art of blessing! He shared the following stories with me the last time we met.

Mahmoudou met a woman who was absolutely desperate about her teenaged son who drank, smoked, used drugs, and had a knife he was constantly threatening people with. She was afraid of her own son. Mahmoudou told her simply to bless him at different times of the day. She did. One day, her son came to her and confessed he was fed up with the life he was living. From one day to another, he radically changed his behavior, even attended daily prayers at the local mosque, to the extent that neighbors could hardly believe the change

Mahmoudou's second story involved a rivalry among co-spouses of a husband. In Africa, these rivalries can be unbelievably ferocious. The women have spells cast on each other and put herbs in a co-spouse's dish the evening she is meant to spend the night with the husband to make him impotent, to mention but a few malicious acts they do. Africans are also extraordinarily receptive to the practice of blessing, because their minds are far less cluttered by all sorts of theories and views than our Western minds are. In the present case, a first wife was being harassed and beaten by the husband and pestered by the new younger co-spouse and was utterly desperate. Mahmoudou told her to simply bless the husband and co-wife. The very next day, the husband came to ask forgiveness for the way he had been treating her, and the two wives are now given as a model of harmony in the whole neighborhood.

A participant of my workshops, Andrée, had decided to leave her husband following serious problems in the relationship. After her departure, her husband started calling her daily, sometimes two or three times the same day. He became more and more verbally violent, to the point that Andrée became really fearful. She then took my workshop on blessing and started blessing her spouse. She wrote a long blessing that expressed deep gratitude for all of her husband's positive qualities, which she prayed and pondered upon every day.

After just a few days of blessing, the phone calls abruptly stopped, and later her husband called to present excuses for his earlier behavior. As a preparation for their appearance in court, Andrée blessed her husband, the judge, the lawyers, the space of the court building. Whereas earlier in her life, such an experience would have almost destroyed her, she stayed calm throughout the proceedings, and everything proceeded harmoniously.

A woman from Geneva called to tell me the following story. She had just read the book on blessing and was at the supermarket when a woman next to her erupted into a long, racist tirade against Africans. First she was shocked, and then she remembered the practice of blessing and started silently blessing this woman. After a brief moment, she went over to examine a collection of crystals. Two minutes later, the other woman, with whom not a single word had been exchanged, came to make amends for the racist remarks she had made.

Natalia's son and his wife were childless, and modern medicine had not been able to help. They were desperate, and the wife sometimes cried at family reunions. Then Natalia discovered *The Gentle Art of Blessing*. She immediately started blessing the young couple in every imaginable way, including their bodies. The next month, the wife became pregnant and later gave birth to a beautiful boy. Without knowing anything about my book or Natalia's blessings for them, they named their son Pierre.

Some scientists will of course interject that there is no proof that Natalia's blessings had anything to do with the pregnancy. To that I would reply two things. First, when for twenty years I have heard of healings of many different kinds of situations through this practice, by people of all walks of life from Eskimo grandmothers (see "Letters and Emails") to CEOs and the barely literate, I cannot continue believing in chance as the dictionary defines it. Rather, chance becomes "God's way of staying anonymous," as a frequently heard statement says.

But more fundamentally, it has been argued that modern science cannot really prove anything, in the sense of giving a definite and certain explanation of how something happens. To really prove anything, we would have to hold all the variables in an experiment constant, and that is strictly impossible, as there are hundreds or even thousands of potential variables in any experiment. For instance, when testing new pharmaceutical drugs, no company has taken into consideration the thought processes and beliefs of those who make, prescribe, and sell the drugs, not to mention those of the consumers. Yet these might very well be the most important factors in a drug's efficiency, as various recent experiments and a vast literature on placebos suggest. So, even in a laboratory, we never have absolute proof, only a temporary working hypothesis, as the Newton of the twentieth century—Stephen Hawking—once observed.

Personally, I prefer living my life with the temporary working hypothesis that blessing is a spiritual law that heals, because (1) it makes those who practice it so joyful and happy to live in a blessing state of mind, (2) I and so many others have consistently observed that it works, and (3) it certainly doesn't harm anyone! Imagine a world where everyone spent their time blessing. You can't help but believe it would be a better place!

Cosette was a gorgeous eighteen-year-old participant in one of my summer workshops. Earlier that year, she had been invited by a good school friend of hers, John, to his apartment in the company of another boy she knew less well. Once they arrived, the other fellow attempted to rape her, with the full consent of John. She managed to avoid the worst but was terribly traumatized by the experience, and she immediately cut off all relations with her friend John.

During the workshop, she shared this traumatic experience, and the scars were still very evident. We spoke simply about blessing John and his friend, and I wrote out a short blessing for her. A few weeks later, after she had diligently applied the practice of blessing, out of the blue John phoned her and apologized sincerely for what had happened.

Possibly the most beautiful story of a relationship healed by blessing was shared with me by my dear friend Mahmoudou, who runs a small nongovernmental organization (NGO) that works with over twelve thousand women in the Mopti region of Mali, West Africa—some of the poorest rural women in the world.

Ahmed had developed a grudge against his younger brother Karim because he had refused to sell some bags of rice to his elder brother for his third marriage. Over a period of ten years, Ahmed expressed growing hostility toward his younger brother, even threatening him with a knife. The situation became so tense, the family asked Karim to leave the village where he lived with his elder brother, and he went to the small town of Mopti where Mahmoudou lives. One day, Ahmed came to Mopti, presumably to kill him because he shot Karim while he was eating. Ahmed missed Karim's heart, injuring his shoulder. The elder brother was arrested by the police, and Karim did all he could to free him, even selling his TV so his elder brother could be released on bail. When Ahmed was freed, he swore he would kill his younger brother.

Karim asked Mahmoudou what he could do. Mahmoudou suggested he simply bless his brother three or four times a day. He added that Karim might at the same time bless all those who were filled with hate like Ahmed. (This step, which I call the universalization of blessing, is precious because it tends to impersonalize the evil or error being manifested. We are not only blessing a person but contributing to the healing of a universal condition affecting mankind in general, in this case anger and hatred.)

Two months later, Mahmoudou returned from a trip, and Karim came to his home at 2 AM because he was so eager to share what had happened. Only ten days after he started blessing Ahmed, a delegation of four people came from the village to present Ahmed's excuses for the way he had treated his brother in the past years. Karim returned to the village, and now his brother does not miss a single opportunity to be of service to his younger brother. People could hardly believe such a longstanding feud could end so abruptly.

Maria, another participant of my summer workshops, was the second wife of a talented artist. The artist's first marriage, from which he had three children, had ended in a divorce because of his unfaithfulness. At the time of the divorce, the law was extremely severe with the unfaithful spouse, and he not only had to pay for the upkeep and schooling of his children but a pension for life for his first wife, despite the fact that she had a job.

The children visited the father two to three times a year. When they were at their father's home, they were civil, but when they met elsewhere, the children didn't even acknowledge the existence of their father let alone of his second wife. Relations with the former wife approximated temperatures of Northern Siberia in January!

Maria decided she would give blessing a try. And the next summer, she shared in the workshop the miracle that had happened: not only had the relations with the children been completely transformed, but for the father's sixtieth birthday, his former wife sent him a friendly letter and informed him that he no longer needed to pay the pension he owed her!

At the fifteenth-anniversary ceremonies of my British publisher, Cygnus Books, British writer Diana Cooper, a specialist on Atlantis, shared with me the following beautiful healing of total paralysis by blessing:

A man had been involved in a serious accident out of which he emerged totally paralyzed. He could only move one little finger, and the doctors had predicted a life of permanent and total disablement. He decided he would spend his time blessing his only mobile limb—his finger! He just spent the whole day blessing it. Soon, a second finger started moving. He added it to his blessings. Then a third, then the whole hand. Little by little, he regained the use of his whole body.

Since writing this book in French in 1997, the dimension of blessing as an expression of gratitude is coming forth more and more forcefully for me. And I truly believe that gratitude is the most powerful mental tool we have at our disposal for completely avoiding the victim mentality, for constantly seeing the cup half full rather than half empty, for keeping our joy intact—and the world certainly needs our joy in these times of immense turbulence. This gratitude comes out often in the following letters and emails about blessing.

LETTERS AND EMAILS

"It is some years now that I have been practicing the gentle art of blessing and how I am grateful about it. Blessings make life lighter and sweeter. No anger can resist blessing, and resentment turns into gentleness," wrote Jeanne of Aix-en-Provence, France.

A young Syrian artist, Rime, wrote that, for her, the book "enables me to understand that I have nothing to lose, nothing to fear, that the only thing that matters is *love*. I have started practicing blessing, and it is something so wonderful that has entered my life."

I regularly share this practice at the local Geneva prison, Champ-Dollon, where I work as a volunteer visitor. (The great majority of the inmates are foreigners and have no family in Switzerland.) A Liberian inmate I am visiting now has started systematically blessing inmates and guards, and it is profoundly changing his vision of his world.

Another young inmate imprisoned for murder, Bernard, wrote,

> *Your book is a marvel. It is opening my eyes on so many things and day-by-day enables me to live life with joy. Since reading the book, I bless all and everything nonstop. I have the impression it is bearing fruit and that makes me very happy. I am going to make photocopies of the text "The Gentle Art of Blessing" in the first chapter of the book and share it with as many inmates as possible. For if everyone practiced it, everything would change so rapidly.*

A retired French school teacher, Josette, wrote me a four-page letter explaining how she has made praise and blessing into a way of life, of thinking, just like the Jesus Prayer of many Russian mystics. Her constant prayer is, "I praise Thee, God of Love, in my brother (or in the rain, in the flowers …). I thank Thee for … [name]. May she/he be blessed and welcome Thy peace."

She also wrote, "A warm handshake accompanied by a blessing made sincerely and with an alert consciousness bring with them life and peace. Such praise and blessing accompany all my greetings and expressions of politeness, and I am careful to anchor them solidly in the now."

Tania from Canada wrote, "Once more, I have to thank you: in my complicated life, your book is a source of strength, joy, forgiveness, and blessings for me and others. It enabled me to help friends who were 'stuck' in their negativity and suffering."

In an earlier email, she had shared how she was involved in some very painful litigation with people everyone described as nasty hooligans and swindlers without a conscience:

In the past weeks, I have been practicing blessing at different moments of the day for all those I love, but especially toward these "enemies." And in the past days, we won the "battle." They suddenly became aware of our good faith, our lack of animosity, and they changed their standpoint. Tonight, the day after Thanksgiving, I thank God for the extraordinary power of blessing. Your book is on my night table, and every day I realize more clearly how much easier it is to bless than to curse—and how the universe reacts better.

In still another email she described how a friend of hers who was facing a dangerous dental problem was healed through blessing.

An African reader, Jean-Jacques, wrote from Burkina Faso,

I reread your book at least four times and I never have enough of it. There has been a major change in my daily life. Before, my heart used to be filled with bitterness toward those who offended me. My face was constantly tense and expressed dissatisfaction. The art of blessing has freed me from many bad things. I am relaxed and smile, there is peace in my heart, and when I meet someone, I bless them and this makes me feel so good. Even my sleep has improved! It has not been difficult. Whenever someone insults or criticizes me, I bless them silently, and a fountain of peace and goodness rises from the wellspring of my heart.

A friend who directed a large hotel and an NGO for the rehabilitation of abused children wrote, "Your book replies at last to questions I had been asking myself for years. Since I have read it, an intense joy inhabits me."

Another African reader wrote from Mali,

Never has my financial situation been as difficult. Yet never have I been so happy. I swear and take Allah as witness that each time I bless a problem, it disappears! I am constantly filled with joy, overflowing with something I find difficult to describe but which is totally satisfying. Whenever I bless, I feel that I am supported by a Presence that watches over me, guides me, counsels me, surrounds me with a protective barrier, gives me direction.

Valentina, who works as a nurse on a Navajo reservation in Arizona, wrote,

If we do not try [blessing] we will not know.
For all those ailing in the world
Until their every sickness has been healed,
May I myself become for them
The doctor, the nurse, the medicine itself.
We can become such medicine through blessing.

I quote rather extensively from the following email received from Caroline in England, as it makes an important point about blessing. She wrote about a bad tooth infection for which she had tried almost everything, including antibiotics, which didn't seem to work either.

I was in tears with the pain. I asked for an angel . . . and a prayer. Then I went up to bed and immediately saw your book, which a friend had given me recently but I hadn't started reading yet, so I began. And then things started to change.

It makes so much sense for me. I have always had trouble with the idea of forgiveness. I know I should be able to forgive, but how do you do it? It is never explained in the spiritual traditions; we are just supposed to know that we must forgive and how to do so. But there was always a missing part for me—and this book has helped me to find that at last. Because I realize that it is not so much about forgiving, which makes me feel I must somehow let go of the pain I feel over something. It is more about transforming those feelings and replacing them with new ones that simply allow the hurt to dissolve into the background.

When we bless people, it immediately transforms any ill-will we may have towards them, rather than trying to "forgive" and then feeling bad in ourselves because it is so difficult to do! And when we bless it also renders it completely unnecessary to delve into all of our own damaged feelings, or to have to make meaning from painful experiences.

When we bless, all the rest just seems to dissolve! It seems to simply stop our own negativity in its tracks.

I tried it today, and as I read the book it began to confirm what I was starting to feel about my tooth infection, which was that the healing would come when I could begin to move outwards from myself, rather than being so deeply focused on my own pain. I found myself just blessing everyone I knew, those I loved, those I didn't love so much—everyone! I blessed my tooth and the pain it was bringing me because I am learning from it. . . . And the infection has already changed, not gone but changed, and I feel lighter in myself.

I think the Art of Blessing is a very powerful tool for healing and transformation.

Michael, an inmate from death row in Texas, wrote to a friend of mine who had sent him the book:

I loved the book and lent it to friends who were as touched as I was. It is true that if we lived constantly blessing, the world would know more peace. I already caught myself blessing those who make me angry. It eliminates a great deal of stress and frustration and replaces these feelings by peace and a feeling of calm.

Delice, an Alutiiq Eskimo from Afognak Island, Alaska, wrote, "Thank you for your blessing. What you wrote was beautiful. Reading your words brought my deceased folks, aunties, and grandmother close to me again. Whatever happens, thank you."

An American teenager, Hilly, in her application to enter college, wrote the following, which especially rejoiced me because it shows that we can start blessing at a very young age, with immediate results:

I started to bless individuals I encountered throughout my day. I didn't always know them and certainly didn't always admire them, yet I just silently, and sincerely, began blessing them. I challenged myself to find something to bless in those I may not have looked favorably upon before, and it became obvious to me that whatever judgment and contempt I was holding on to myself was more harmful to me than to the objects of my disdain. Blessing quickly transformed itself into joy, becoming more and more natural as I blessed everyone I saw. While those I blessed never sent thank yous or gifts, I became aware of the many blessings in my own life. I no longer wasted energy on negativity or animosity and let positive thoughts control my mind-set. With my newfound compassion for others, my life began to reflect my renewed attitude. The rewards I have received, and continue to receive, since discovering the gentle art of blessing know no bounds. I never could have imagined that something as simple as a silent blessing could change my life. This book has given me a renewed sense of compassion, in a time when kindness and grace towards others are not often cherished as they should be.

Nancy wrote this about the text on blessing: "It is the most understandable description of what blessing is all about I have read. I honestly feel that now I know what it means to bless someone. Until I read your text, I only said the words. I always wondered what it means to give and receive a blessing."

Perla in the Philippines emailed,

I shared [this practice] with my mother and she was so touched by it that she asked me to print out ten copies for her friends. I thought it was such a great idea I made eighty copies to send out with our Christmas cards. I have also been sending it out in email form to friends all round the world. . . . With the power of email, I believe that many more people will practice and share this art. You have started something beautiful with the words that you share online. I believe that as more and more practice

the art of blessing, the world will truly come to a healing and
wholeness and reach a new level.

A reader who found the text on a spirituality website made this really lovely comment: "Thank you for this text. It met a need and helped me stop an ongoing criticism of others. I am so much happier blessing than judging."

I just love that last comment, don't you? A person whose thought radiates the gentleness of blessing is the first beneficiary of this practice, as anyone can verify for himself.

Of the innumerable responses I have received over the past twenty years, few have rejoiced me as much as the following, because it is so fundamental to the deeper understanding of blessing: "This text made me realize that I cannot hope to enter the Kingdom of God if I do not take the whole world with me." These are just a few brief excerpts from so many more messages. Ultimately, the basic theme of these letters is:

> *Blessing works!*
> *Blessing heals!*
> *Blessing fills life with joy, vitality,*
> *   and gratitude.*
> *Blessing is love in action.*

By purchasing this book, you have already started blessing, without even being aware of it!

Half of the author's royalties from this book will be donated to the Women's World Summit Foundation of Geneva (*www.woman.ch*), a remarkable organization doing important humanitarian work worldwide. Your purchase will be a blessing to women and children on the whole planet. "When the mouths of the ants get together, they can carry an elephant," says a Mossi African proverb. Replace *mouth* with *purse* and you will have an idea of what we mean.

With the exception of a part-time assistant, this foundation is entirely run by volunteers, including its founder-director. Its overhead is extremely low, especially given the quality and impact of its activities. Above all, it is run in a rare spirit of compassion, expressing great creativity and innovative approaches. The foundation's activities are in the field of women's and children's rights and development goals promised by world leaders. More specifically, the foundation has:

- Created the unique Prize for Women's Creativity in Rural Life, which is given yearly to creative women at the grass roots around the world. Over a period of eighteen years, close to 350 women in over a hundred countries have received the prize. For the first time, the humblest, most hardworking women on the planet are acknowledged for their outstanding contribution to human well-being. Five hundred million of them survive on a dollar a day, and many raise their families alone, often walking miles for wood and water.

- Spearheaded the creation of World Rural Women's Day, which falls on October 15 each year. Thanks to the Foundation's untiring efforts, this has now become an official United Nations day and been recognized by a series of countries around the world, including the United States.

🍁 Launched World Day for the Prevention of Child Abuse, which occurs on November 19 each year. As of 2008, it had enlisted close to one thousand institutions and NGOs in 135 countries to fight child abuse in the sexual field, especially pedophilia.

🍁 Created a world prize for innovative activities in the field of child abuse prevention.

SUGGESTED READING

Aurobindo, Sri. *Bhagavad Gita in the Light of Sri Aurobindo*. Edited by Maheshwar. Pondichery, India: Sri Aurobindo Press, 1992.

Bâ, Amadou Hampaté. *Vie et enseignement de Tierno Bokar, le sage de Bandiagara*. Paris: Seuil, 1980.

Barbour, Julian B. *The End of Time: The Next Revolution in Our Understanding of the Universe*. London: Phoenix, 2000.

The Bible. New Revised Standard Version. Grand Rapids, Mich.: Zondervan, 1989.

Boyle, Patton. *Screaming Hawk: Flying Eagle's Training of a Mystic Warrior*. New York: Station Hill Press, 1994.

Brother Lawrence. *The Practice of the Presence of God*. Transl. by Robert Edmonson. Orleans, Mass.: Paraclete Press, 1984.

Burke, Richard M. *Cosmic Consciousness: A Study in the Evolution of the Human Mind*. New York: Dutton, 1969.

Buttrick, George A. *The Interpreter's Bible*. Nashville, Tenn.: Abingdon Press, 1952.

Chittick, William C. *The Sufi Path of Love: The Spiritual Teachings of Rumi*. Albany: State University of New York Press, 1983.

Chopra, Deepak. *Unconditional Life: Mastering the Forces that Shape Personal Reality*. New York: Random House Audio, 1991.

CSPS. *A Century of Christian Science Healing, 1866–1966*. Boston: Christian Science Publishing Society, 1966.

Delumeau, Jean. *Le péché et la peur. La culpabilisation en Occident XIIIᵉ-XVIIIᵉ siècles*. Paris: Fayard, 1983.

Dominguez, Joe and Vicki Robin. *Your Money or Your Life: Transforming Your Relationship with Money and Achieving Financial Independence*. New York: Viking, 1992.

Easwaran, Eknath. *Passage Meditation: Bringing the Deep Wisdom of the Heart into Daily Life*. Tomales, Calif.: Nilgiri Press, 2008.

Eddy, Mary Baker. "Christian Healing." In *Prose Works Other Than Science or Health*. Boston: Christian Science Publishing Society, 1985.

———. *Science and Health with Key to the Scriptures*. Study ed. Boston: Christian Science Publishing Society, 2006.

Ferrucci, Piero. *Inevitable Grace*. Los Angeles: J. P. Tarcher, 1990.

Foundation for Inner Peace. *A Course in Miracles*. London: Arkana Paperbacks, 1985.

Gibran, Kahlil. *The Prophet*. New York: Heinemann, 1926.

Goldstein, Martin, and Inge F. Goldstein. *How We Know: An Exploration of the Scientific Process*. New York: Da Capo Press, 1978.

Hamilton, Craig. "Scientific Proof of the Existence of God." *What Is Enlightenment?*, Spring–Summer 1997. Periodical now called *Enlightenment Magazine*.

Hardy, Alister. *The Spiritual Nature of Man: A Study of Contemporary Religious Experience*. Oxford: Clarendon Press, 1979.

Hawkins, David R. *Power vs. Force: The Hidden Determinants of Human Behavior*. West Sedona, Ariz.: Veritas Publishing, 1995.

Holmstrom, John. *When Prayers Are Answered*. New York: Perigee Books, 1995.

Jampolsky, Gerald G. *Love Is Letting Go of Fear*. New York: Bantam, 1979.

————. *Forgiveness: The Greatest Healer of All*. Hillsboro, Ore.: Beyond Words Publishing, 1999.

Johnston, William, ed. *The Cloud of Unknowing and the Book of Privy Counseling*. New York: Image Books, 1996.

Julian. *Enfolded in Love: Daily Readings with Julian of Norwich*. London: Darton, Longman and Todd, Ltd., 1980.

Kabat-Zinn, Jon. *Mindfulness Meditation for Everyday Life*. New York: Hyperion, 1994.

Katie, Byron. *A Thousand Names for Joy: Living in Harmony with the Way Things Are*. New York: Random House, 2007.

Kuhn, Thomas. *The Structure of Scientific Revolutions*. Chicago: University of Chicago Press, 1992.

Mandela, Nelson. *Long Walk to Freedom*. London: Abacus, 1995.

Matthews, Caitlín. *The Little Book of Celtic Blessings*. Shaftesbury, Dorset, UK: Element Books, 1994.

Meier, Käte. "Tu aimeras ton prochain comme toi-même." *The Herald of Christian Science*, French edition, January 1993, 3–5.

Myrdal, Gunnar. *Objectivity in Social Research*. New York, Pantheon, 1969.

Peel, Doris. "Song for the New Year." *The Christian Science Monitor*, December 31, 1960.

Phillips, J. B. *The New Testament in Modern English*. New York: Macmillan, 1969.

Pradervand, Pierre. *Listening to Africa: Developing Africa from the Grassroots*. New York: Praeger, 1989.

Rinpoche, Dugpa. *Préceptes de Vie*. Paris: Ed. du Châtelet, 1996.

Ritchie, George G., and Elisabeth Sherrill. *Return from Tomorrow*. Old Tappan, N.J.: Spire Books, 1981.

Siegel, Bernie S. M.D. *Love, Medicine & Miracles: Lessons Learned about Self-healing from a Surgeon's Experience with Exceptional Patients*. New York: Harper and Row, 1986.

Spangler, David. *Blessing: The Art and the Practice*. New York: Riverhead Books, 2002.

Stauffer, Edith. *Unconditional Love and Forgiveness*. Burbank, Calif.: Triangle Publications, 1987.

Steinsaltz, Adin. *La rose aux treize pétales: Introduction à la Cabbale*. Paris: Albin Michel, 1996 (translated from the French edition).

Tolle, Eckhart. *The Power of Now*. Novato, Calif.: New World Library, 1999.

Tolstoy, Leo. *Twenty-Three Tales*. London: Oxford University Press, 1960.

Zukav, Gary. *The Dancing Wu Li Masters: An Overview of the New Physics*. New York: Bantam, 1980.